A Decade of Debt

Carmen M. Reinhart and
Kenneth S. Rogoff

PETERSON INSTITUTE FOR INTERNATIONAL ECONOMICS
Washington, DC
September 2011

Carmen M. Reinhart is the Dennis Weatherstone Senior Fellow at the Peterson Institute for International Economics. She was previously professor of economics and director of the Center for International Economics at the University of Maryland. She was chief economist and vice president at the investment bank Bear Stearns in the 1980s and spent several years at the International Monetary Fund. She is a research associate at the National Bureau of Economic Research, research fellow at the Centre for Economic Policy Research, and member of the Congressional Budget Office Panel of Economic Advisers and Council on Foreign Relations. She has served on many editorial boards and has frequently testified before Congress. Reinhart's work has helped to inform the understanding of financial crises for over a decade. Her numerous papers on macroeconomics, international finance, and trade have been published in leading scholarly journals. She is the recipient of the 2010 TIAA-CREF Paul A. Samuelson Award. Her best-selling book (with Kenneth S. Rogoff) entitled *This Time is Different: Eight Centuries of Financial Folly*, which has been translated into 13 languages, documents the striking similarities of the recurring booms and busts that have characterized financial history. She received her PhD from Columbia University.

Kenneth S. Rogoff is a member of the Peterson Institute for International Economics Advisory Committee and the Thomas D. Cabot Professor of Public Policy and Professor of Economics at Harvard University. He also served as chief economist and director of research at the International Monetary Fund (2001–03). He is the recipient of the 2010 TIAA-CREF Paul A. Samuelson Award. His publications include *This Time is Different: Eight Centuries of Financial Folly*, *Handbook of International Economics* Volume III, and *Foundations of International Macroeconomics*. Rogoff is a frequent commentator for NPR, the *Wall Street Journal*, and the *Financial Times*.

PETER G. PETERSON INSTITUTE FOR INTERNATIONAL ECONOMICS
1750 Massachusetts Avenue, NW
Washington, DC 20036-1903
(202) 328-9000   FAX: (202) 659-3225
www.piie.com

C. Fred Bergsten, *Director*
Edward A. Tureen, *Director of Publications, Marketing, and Web Development*

Printing by United Book Press, Inc.

Printed in the United States of America.

13 12 11   5 4 3 2

Library of Congress Cataloging-in-Publication Data

Reinhart, Carmen M.
  A decade of debt / Carmen M. Reinhart and Kenneth S. Rogoff.
    p. cm.
  Includes bibliographical references and index.
  ISBN 978-0-88132-622-2
  1. Debts, Public. 2. Finance, Public. I. Rogoff, Kenneth S. II. Title.
  HJ8015.R45 2011
  336.3'4--dc23

                              2011024349

Contents

Tables

Figures

Boxes

Preface

This Policy Analysis addresses a fundamentally new feature of the contemporary world economy: the simultaneous peacetime buildup of very large public debt positions in virtually all of the advanced high-income countries. The recent financial crisis sharply accelerated this fiscal deterioration but it was already well underway in some countries, including the United States, where demographic prospects had posed extremely worrisome trajectories for a number of years.

This study has three basic purposes. First, it quantifies the recent surge of debt positions in the advanced countries over the past decade and places it in a historical context. Second, it notes the association between high public debt with a series of key economic variables, including growth rates and the risks of debt restructurings and defaults. Third, it stresses the possibility of a return to the financial repression practiced by many governments in earlier periods to cope with previous debt buildups.

The paper concludes that debt profiles in most advanced and some emerging economies have grown to dangerous and unsustainable levels and that major changes are therefore required in projected spending and revenue levels. Critical questions raised by this prognosis include the likely nature and timing of new crises, and hence the policy strategies that countries should undertake to prevent such outcomes without jeopardizing recovery from the Great Recession.

The study is authored by Carmen Reinhart and Kenneth Rogoff, drawing on their definitive study of the history of debt in *This Time is Different: Eight Centuries of Financial Folly*. Dr. Reinhart is the new Dennis Weatherstone Senior Fellow at the Peterson Institute for International Economics, having joined our staff in November 2010. She is the recipient of the 2010 TIAA-CREF

Paul A. Samuelson Award. Dr. Rogoff is the Thomas D. Cabot Professor of Public Policy and Professor of Economics at Harvard University, and was Chief Economist and Director of Research at the International Monetary Fund during 2001–03. An earlier version of the study was released as Working Paper 16827 of the National Bureau of Economic Research, of which Dr. Reinhart and Dr. Rogoff are associates.

The Institute undertook this project at the request of the Peter G. Peterson Foundation, which is a completely separate entity. The Foundation focuses much of its attention on the fiscal prospects and problems of the United States, and asked the Institute to imbed those national issues in the global context to assess how that broader perspective might affect the outlook and especially the need for early policy action by the United States. This project follows on two earlier studies that we conducted at the request of Foundation: *The Global Outlook for Government Debt over the Next 25 Years*, by Joseph E. Gagnon and Marc Hinterschweiger, and *The Long-Term International Economic Position of the United States*, which I edited and we released as Special Report 20 in May 2009.

The Peter G. Peterson Institute for International Economics is a private, nonprofit institution for the study and discussion of international economic policy. Its purpose is to analyze important issues in that area and to develop and communicate practical new approaches for dealing with them. The Institute is completely nonpartisan.

The Institute is funded by a highly diversified group of philanthropic foundations, private corporations, and interested individuals. About 35 percent of the Institute's resources in our latest fiscal year was provided by contributors outside the United States. This study, as noted, was supported by the Peter G. Peterson Foundation.

The Institute's Board of Directors bears overall responsibilities for the Institute and gives general guidance and approval to its research program, including the identification of topics that are likely to become important over the medium run (one to three years) and that should be addressed by the Institute. The director, working closely with the staff and outside Advisory Committee, is responsible for the development of particular projects and makes the final decision to publish an individual study.

The Institute hopes that its studies and other activities will contribute to building a stronger foundation for international economic policy around the world. We invite readers of these publications to let us know how they think we can best accomplish this objective.

C. FRED BERGSTEN
Director
August 2011

Acknowledgments

The authors are grateful to C. Fred Bergsten, Joseph Gagnon, Peter G. Peterson, Vincent R. Reinhart, and participants at a meeting at the Peterson Foundation on September 27, 2010 for helpful comments, suggestions, and discussions, to National Science Foundation Grant No. 0849224 for financial support, and to Maura Francese, Elín Guðjónsdóttir, Fregert Gustaffson, Sophia Lazaretou, Ashok Mody, Diego Saravia, and Jan-Luiten Van Zanden for providing invaluable references on individual countries and, in some cases, sharing their historical data as well.

Executive Summary

This Policy Analysis presents evidence that public debts in the advanced economies have surged in recent years to levels not recorded since the end of World War II, surpassing the heights reached during the World War I and the Great Depression. At the same time, private debt levels, particularly those of financial institutions and households, are in uncharted territory and are (in varying degrees) a contingent liability of the public sector in many countries. Historically, high leverage episodes have been associated with slower economic growth and a higher incidence of default or, more generally, restructuring of public and private debts. A more subtle form of debt restructuring in the guise of "financial repression" (which had its heyday during the tightly regulated Bretton Woods system) also importantly facilitated sharper and more rapid debt reduction than would have otherwise been the case from the late 1940s to the 1970s. It is conjectured here that the pressing needs of governments to reduce debt rollover risks and curb rising interest expenditures in light of the substantial debt overhang (combined with the widespread "official aversion" to explicit restructuring) are leading to a revival of financial repression—including more directed lending to government by captive domestic audiences (such as pension funds), explicit or implicit caps on interest rates, and tighter regulation on cross-border capital movements.

A Decade of Debt

CARMEN M. REINHART AND KENNETH S. ROGOFF

I. Introduction

Public debts in the advanced economies have surged in recent years to levels that have not been recorded since the end of World War II. Through 2010, the average public debt/GDP ratio for all the advanced economies has surpassed the pre-World War II peaks reached during the World War I and subsequently during the Great Depression.[1] Private debt levels, particularly those of financial institutions and households, are similarly in uncharted territory and represent (in varying degrees) potential contingent liability of the public sector in many countries, including the United States.

As documented in Reinhart, Rogoff, and Savastano (2003) for emerging-market countries, large public debt overhangs do not unwind quickly and seldom painlessly. In particular, debt-to-GDP ratios are seldom reduced entirely through consistent robust economic growth. More commonly, reducing debt levels significantly has relied on fiscal austerity, debt restructuring (sometimes outright default), or a combination of these.

---

1. Unless otherwise noted, public debt in this Policy Analysis refers to gross central government debt. As such, it does not include other levels of government indebtedness (for example, state and local debt in the United States), nor does it encompass public enterprise debt, or debt that carries an explicit (let alone implicit) government guarantee. Contingent liabilities of the government associated with Social Security benefits are not incorporated in our long (a century or, for some countries, more) of government debt data and its analysis. Domestic public debt is government debt issued under domestic legal jurisdiction. Public debt does not include obligations carrying a government guarantee. Total gross external debt includes the external debts of *all* branches of government as well as private debt issued by domestic private entities under a foreign jurisdiction.

In a complementary analysis of private debt deleveraging episodes following systemic financial crises, Reinhart and Reinhart (2011) show that the debt reduction process goes on for an average of about seven years. Also, because of declining output and accumulating arrears on existing debts, private debt ratios usually continue to climb even until two or three years after the height of the financial crisis—delaying the effective reduction of debt ratios.[2]

The combination of high and climbing public debts (a rising share of which is held by major central banks) and the protracted process of private deleveraging makes it likely that the ten years from 2008 to 2017 will be aptly described as a decade of debt. As such, the issues we raise in this Policy Analysis will weigh heavily on the public policy agenda of numerous advanced economies and global financial markets for some time to come. The following summarizes key aspects of our recent body of work on public debt and financial crises. Of course, if global real interest rates remain very low for an extended period, carrying costs of debt will be correspondingly low, and exceptionally high leverage ratios can persist longer than usual. However, as we emphasize in Reinhart and Rogoff (2009), interest rates can turn far faster than debt levels, so if deleveraging does not occur, debt will be a continuing vulnerability. The analysis that follows draws on and expands various strands of our earlier work.[3]

Historically, high leverage episodes have been associated with slower economic growth. This observation applies to the high-debt episodes that follow on the heels of wars as well as to their peacetime counterparts. It also characterizes episodes where high debt levels were not associated with markedly higher interest rates.[4]

Surges in private debt lead to private defaults (which most often become manifest in the form of banking crises).[5] Banking crises are associated with mounting public debt, which ultimately lead to a higher incidence of sovereign default or, more generally, restructuring of public and private debts.

---

2. Private deleveraging, as measured by new borrowing (see Fostel and Geanokoplos 2008 and Geanokoplos 2009) usually begins to slow down markedly or decline during the crisis and, in some cases, just before the onset of crisis.

3. Specifically, this Policy Analysis draws on Reinhart and Rogoff (2008, 2009, 2010a, 2010b, 2011a, 2011b). Although much of this Policy Analysis is devoted to synthesizing earlier work, there is important new material here, including the discussion of how World War I and Great Depression debt were largely resolved through outright default and restructuring, whereas World War II debts were often resolved through financial repression. We argue that financial repression is likely to play a big role in the exit strategy from the current buildup. We also highlight here the extraordinary external debt levels of Ireland and Iceland compared with all historical norms in our database.

4. See Gagnon and Hinterschweiger (2011) for an analysis of the links between debt and interest rates.

5. See Kaminsky and Reinhart (1999).

Specifically, banking crises and surges in public debt help to "predict" sovereign debt crises. Of course, this historical pattern had been dominant prior to the era of mega bailouts ushered in with the 1992 Japanese domestic banking crisis, followed by (on an international scale) the 1994–95 Mexican peso crises, reinforced during the Asian crisis with the Korean package, and reaching ever-escalating historic highs on both domestic and international dimensions at the time of this writing. The "bailout approach" in the current episode began in the summer of 2007 in the United States in response to the subprime mortgage crisis and morphed into the most serious advanced-economy debt crisis since the 1930s.

A more subtle form of debt restructuring takes the form of "financial repression" (which had its heyday during the tightly regulated Bretton Woods system). Limiting investment choices of the private sector importantly facilitated sharper and more rapid debt reduction from the late 1940s to the 1970s than would have otherwise been the case (Reinhart and Sbrancia 2011). We conjecture here that the pressing needs of governments to reduce debt roll-over risks and curb rising interest expenditures in light of the substantial debt overhang, combined with an aversion to more explicit restructuring, may lead to a revival of financial repression. This includes more directed lending to government by captive domestic audiences (such as pension funds), explicit or implicit caps on interest rates, and tighter regulation on cross-border capital movements.[6] A less generous depiction of financial repression (see definition in box 1.1) would include the savaging of pension funds.

Section II places the recent surge in government debt in the advanced economies in historical perspective, distinguishing the timing and magnitudes of earlier high-debt episodes. Section III summarizes our findings on the temporal causal links between financial crises, rapid surges in public debt, and subsequent sovereign restructuring or outright default. In section IV we document that high debt is associated with slower growth—a relationship that is robust across advanced and emerging markets since World War II, as well an earlier era. The last large wave of sovereign defaults or restructurings in the advanced economies during the early 1930s (outright defaults were confined to the handful of countries on the losing side of World War II) is discussed in section V, which also describes the heavy-handed financial regulation (often referred to as financial repression) that helped rapidly reduce the World War II debt overhang. The concluding section suggests many of the elements of financial repression have already begun to resurface (a trend that is likely to gather momentum in coming years), as governments simultaneously grapple with the difficult choices associated with substantial debt reduction.

---

6. There is a literature on financial repression in emerging-market economies (see Easterly 1989 and Giovannini and Di Melo 1993, for example). However, the Bretton Woods system embraced in 1946 established a system of tightly regulated financial markets based on the three pillars of (1) directed credit; (2) interest rate ceilings; and (3) foreign exchange controls (see box 1.1).

Box 1.1 Financial repression defined

The term financial repression was introduced in the literature by the works of Edward Shaw (1973) and Ronald McKinnon (1973). Subsequently, the term became a way of describing emerging-market financial systems prior to the widespread financial liberalization that began in the 1980 (see Agenor and Montiel 2008 for an excellent discussion of the role of inflation and Giovannini and de Melo 1993 and Easterly 1989 for country-specific estimates). However, as we document in this paper, financial repression was also the norm for advanced economies during the post–World War II period and in varying degrees up through the 1980s. We describe here some of its main features.

Pillars of financial repression

1. Explicit or indirect caps or ceilings on interest rates, particularly (but not exclusively) those on government debts. These interest rate ceilings could be effected through various means, including (1) explicit government regulation (for instance, Regulation Q in the United States prohibited banks from paying interest on demand deposits and capped interest rates on saving deposits); (2) ceilings on banks' lending rates, which were a direct subsidy to the government in cases where it borrowed directly from the banks (via loans rather than securitized debt); and (3) interest rate cap in the context of fixed coupon rate nonmarketable debt or (4) maintained through central bank interest rate targets (often at the directive of the Treasury or Ministry of Finance when central bank independence was limited or nonexistent). Allan Meltzer's (2003) monumental history of the Federal Reserve (volume I) documents the US experience in this regard; Alex Cukierman's (1992) classic on central bank independence provides a broader international context.

(continued on next page)

II. Surges in Public Debt

Throughout the ages and across continents, war has been a recurrent causal force behind rapid deteriorations in government finances and surges in public indebtedness. This pattern shows through in world debt aggregates and individual country histories. Thus, it is not surprising to see that, particularly for the advanced economies, two spikes in debt aggregates correspond to the two world wars (figure 1.1). The smaller set of independent (largely European) economies that populated the globe in the early 1800s experienced a similar sharp run-up in debt during the Napoleonic Wars.

Box 1.1   Financial repression defined *(continued)*

2. Creation and maintenance of a captive domestic audience that facilitated directed credit to the government. This was achieved through multiple layers of regulations from very blunt to more subtle measures. (1) Capital account restrictions and exchange controls orchestrated a "forced home bias" in the portfolio of financial institutions and individuals under the Bretton Woods arrangements. (2) High reserve requirements (usually nonremunerated) as a tax levy on banks (see Brock 1989 for an insightful international comparison). Among more subtle measures, (3) "prudential" regulatory measures requiring that institutions (almost exclusively domestic ones) hold government debts in their portfolios (pension funds have historically been a primary target), (4) transaction taxes on equities (see Campbell and Froot 1994) also act to direct investors toward government (and other) types of debt instruments, and (5) prohibitions on gold transactions.

3. Other common measures associated with financial repression aside from the ones discussed above are (1) direct ownership (e.g., in China or India) of banks or extensive management of banks and other financial institutions (e.g., in Japan) and (2) restricting entry into the financial industry and directing credit to certain industries (see Beim and Calomiris 2000).

Source: Reinhart and Sbrancia (2011) and sources cited therein.

During peacetime, a leading factor behind rapid surges in public debt has been severe or systemic financial crises. With the growing tendency toward increasing government involvement in rescue operations, the link between public debt and financial crashes has become more pronounced in the past two decades or so. More general and chronic fiscal problems (because governments systematically overspend, do not have the political will or ability to tax effectively, or a combination of the two) tend to produce more gradual debt buildups.

As figure 1.1 illustrates, public debts in the advanced economies have surged in recent years to levels not recorded since the end of World War II, surpassing previous peaks reached during World War I and the Great Depression. At the same time, private debt levels, particularly those of households, are simply in uncharted territory and are (in varying degrees) a contingent liability of the public sector in many countries, including the United States. As we emphasize in Reinhart and Rogoff (2009, 2011b) and discuss further below, most governments find it difficult to avoid backstopping significant amounts of private credit during a financial crisis.

**Figure 1.1   Gross central government debt as a percent of GDP:
Advanced and emerging-market economies, 1860–2010**

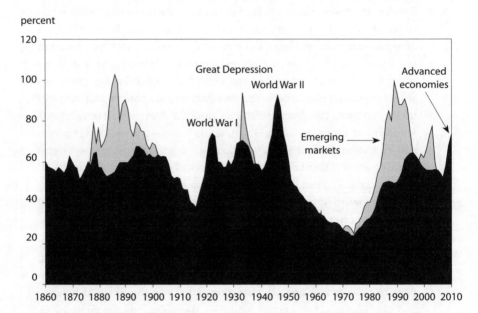

Sources: Reinhart and Rogoff (2011a) and sources cited therein.

Financial Crises and Debt

Figure 1.2 takes advantage of newly unearthed historical data on domestic debt to show the rise in real government debt in the three years following severe banking crises of the 20th century.[7] A buildup in government debt has been a defining characteristic of the aftermath of banking crises for over a century, with government finances deteriorating to produce an average debt rise of 86 percent. This comparative exercise focuses on the percentage increase in debt, rather than the debt-to-GDP ratio, because steep output drops sometimes complicate the interpretation of debt/GDP ratios. As we note in Reinhart and Rogoff (2008), the characteristic huge buildups in government debt are driven mainly by sharp falloffs in tax revenue, owing to the severe and protracted nature of postcrisis recessions. In some famous cases (notably Japan in the 1990s), this deterioration in fiscal balances also owes to surges in government spending to fight the recession. The much ballyhooed bank bailout costs are, in several cases, only a relatively minor contributor to post–financial crisis debt burdens.

---

7. This analysis was first introduced in Reinhart and Rogoff (2008).

Figure 1.2 Cumulative increase in public debt in the three years following systemic banking crisis: Selected post–World War II episodes

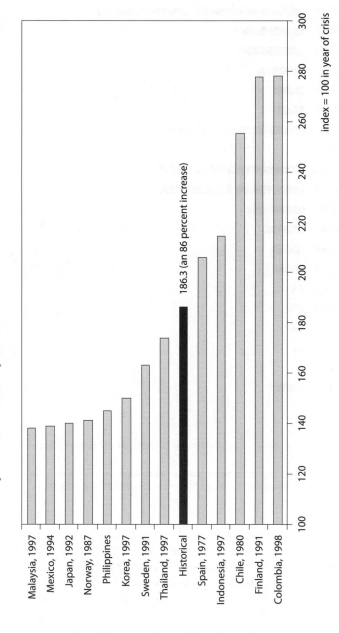

index = 100 in year of crisis

Notes: Each banking crisis episode is identified by country and the beginning year of the crisis. Only major (systemic) banking crisis episodes are included, subject to data limitations. The historical average reported does not include ongoing crisis episodes, which are omitted altogether, as these crises begin in 2007 or later, and debt stock comparison shown is three years after the beginning of the banking crisis.

Source: Reinhart and Rogoff (2008 and 2009) and sources cited therein.

Figure 1.3 Cumulative increase in real public debt since 2007, selected countries

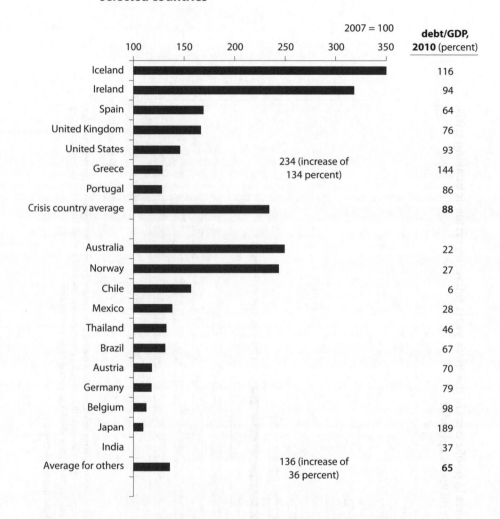

Notes: Unless otherwise noted these figures are for central government debt deflated by consumer prices.

Sources: Prices and nominal GDP from International Monetary Fund, *World Economic Outlook*. For a complete listing of sources for government debt, see Reinhart and Rogoff (2009) and chapter 2.

More broadly, an examination of the aftermath of severe financial crises shows deep and lasting effects on asset prices, output, and employment. Unemployment rises and housing price declines extend out for five and six years, respectively. Even recessions sparked by financial crises do eventually end, albeit almost invariably accompanied by massive increases in government debt.

The 2007–10 Global Buildup in Public Debt

Figure 1.3 illustrates the increase in (inflation adjusted) public debt since 2007. For the countries with systemic financial crises and/or sovereign debt problems (Greece, Iceland, Ireland, Portugal, Spain, the United Kingdom, and the United States), average debt levels are up by about 134 percent, surpassing by a sizable margin the three-year 86 percent benchmark that we find (Reinhart and Rogoff 2009) for earlier deep postwar financial crises. The larger debt buildups in Iceland and Ireland are importantly associated not only with the sheer magnitude of the recessions/depressions in those countries but also with the scale of the bank debt buildup prior to the crisis—which is, as far as we are aware—without parallel in the long history of financial crises. Nor will 2010 (the third year of crisis for Iceland, Ireland, the United Kingdom, and the United States and the second year for the others) be the last year in which rising debt will be recorded. At present, forecasts for the United States show rising debt levels in the foreseeable future; for several others, austerity programs notwithstanding, debts are likely to continue to mount as economic conditions remain subpar and debt servicing costs climb.

Even in countries that did not experience a major financial crisis, debt rose by an average of about 36 percent in real terms between 2007 and 2010.[8] Many economies adopted stimulus packages to deal with the global recession in 2008–09 and were hit by marked declines in government revenues. Moreover, some of the larger increases in debt loads of noncrisis countries (such as Norway, Australia, and Chile) relate to the cyclical downdraft in world commodity prices that accompanied the global recession.

III. The Financial Crash–Sovereign Debt Crisis Sequence

In this section, we summarize the main findings in Reinhart and Rogoff (2011b). Our approach in that paper was to illustrate each main result with both a "big picture" based on cross-country aggregation and a "representative country case study (or studies)" from country histories. Each of the main points highlighted in the figures is complemented by the pertinent debt/GDP-crisis indicator regressions reported at the bottom of each figure. We begin by discussing sovereign default on external debt (that is, when a government defaults on its own external or private-sector debts that were publicly guaranteed).

---

8. Our focus on gross central government debt owes to the fact that time series of broader measures of government debt are not available for many countries. Of course, the true runup in debt is significantly larger than stated here, at least on a present value actuarial basis, due to the extensive government guarantees that have been conferred on the financial sector in the crisis countries and elsewhere, where for example deposit guarantees were raised in 2008.

Figure 1.4   Sovereign default on external debt, total (domestic plus external) public debt, and inflation crises: World aggregates, 1826–2010

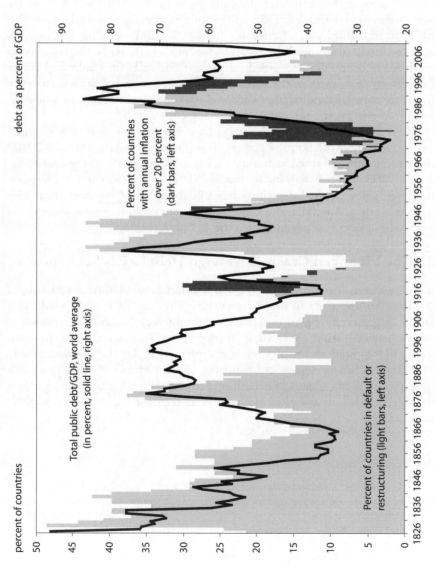

Notes: Unless otherwise noted these figures are for central government debt deflated by consumer prices.

Sources: Prices and nominal GDP from International Monetary Fund, *World Economic Outlook*. For a complete listing of sources for government debt, see Reinhart and Rogoff (2009) and chapter 2.

Table 1.1 Public debt and sovereign default and restructuring: All countries, 1824–2009

Dependent variable	World: Share of countries in default or restructuring	
Sample	1824–2009	
Independent variables	OLS (robust errors)	Logit (robust errors)
World: Public debt/GDP (t-1)	*0.346*	*0.008*
p-value	0	0
Number of observations	184	184
R²	0.224	0.246

OLS = ordinary least squares
Logit = logistic regression

Notes: The debt aggregate for the world is a simple arithmetic average of individual countries' debt/ GDP ratios. For a few countries the time series on debt and exports are much longer dating back to the first half of the 19th century than for nominal GDP. In these cases (Brazil, Canada, Egypt, India, Nicaragua, Thailand, Turkey, and Uruguay) the debt/GDP series was spliced (with appropriate scaling) with the to the available debt/GDP data. The split between advanced and emerging economies is made along the present-day IMF classification.

Sources: Reinhart and Rogoff (2011b), sources cited therein and authors' calculations.

Public Debt Surges and Sovereign Default and Restructuring

Public debt follows a lengthy and repeated boom-bust cycle; the bust phase involves a markedly higher incidence of sovereign debt crises. Public-sector borrowing surges as the crisis nears. In the aggregate, debts continue to rise after default, as arrears accumulate and GDP contracts markedly.[9] Figure 1.4 plots the incidence of external default (lighter bars) from 1826, when the newly independent Latin American economies first entered the global capital market, through 2010 against an unweighted average debt/GDP ratio for all the countries for which such data are available. Upturns in the debt ratio usually precede the rise in default rates, as the regressions (shown in table 1.1) for the world aggregates confirm. Periods of higher indebtedness are also associated with a higher incidence of inflation crises (a more indirect form of default, highlighted as darker bars where the incidence of inflation exceeds that of default). Default through inflation has been more prevalent since World War I, as fiat money became the norm and links to gold severed.

Serial default is a widespread phenomenon across emerging markets and several advanced economies. The most compelling evidence on serial default comes from the individual country histories, shown here for Greece in figure 1.5. The 70 country histories presented in chapter 2 provide broad-based evidence that serial default cut across regions and across time.

---

9. See Reinhart and Rogoff (2009, 2011a) for evidence on output behavior before, during, and after debt crises.

Figure 1.5   Greece: Central government (domestic plus external) debt, default, hyperinflation, and banking crises, 1848–2009

debt as a percent of GDP

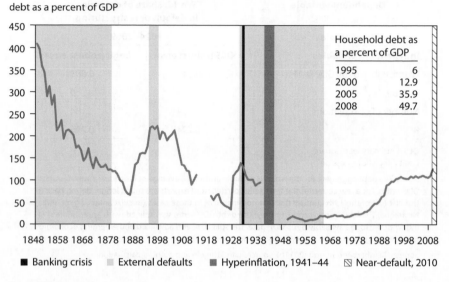

■ Banking crisis   ▨ External defaults   ■ Hyperinflation, 1941–44   ▨ Near-default, 2010

Source: Chapter 2.

The "hallmark" surge in debt on the eve of a debt crisis, banking crisis, or both is quite evident in Greece's last two defaults in 1894 and in 1932—the latter default spell lasted about 33 years from beginning to its eventual resolution in 1964.

Hidden Debts—Private Debts that Become Public

The drama that has most notably engulfed Iceland and Ireland is novel only in the orders of magnitude of the debts, not in the causes and patterns of the crisis.[10] Writing about Chile's crises in the early 1980s, Carlos Diaz-Alejandro (1985) asks us to consider a country that had liberalized its domestic financial sector and was fully integrated into world capital markets.

> The recorded public sector deficit was nonexistent, minuscule, or moderate; the declining importance of ostensible public debt in the national balance sheet was celebrated by some observers.

---

10. Gross external debts ten times the size of GDP (as the cases of Iceland and Ireland) are historically off the charts for both advanced and emerging-market economies. In effect, Reinhart, Rogoff, and Savastano (2003) calculate that more than half of all emerging-market defaults or restructuring episodes since World War II occurred at debt levels of 60 percent or less (which would satisfy the Maastricht criteria).

The private sector was a different matter. Their spending persistently exceeded their income, giving rise to large current account deficits. The current account deficit was financed by large and persistent capital inflows, which is a different way of saying that the domestic largesse was supported by borrowing heavily from the rest of the world. This abundance of foreign capital made it easy for domestic banks to lend liberally to businesses and households. During the credit boom, real estate and equity prices soared—so did debts. Growth seemed inevitable.

However, as Diaz-Alejandro explains, the pity of the boom is that

> little effort was spent on investigating the credentials of new entrants to the ever-growing pool of lenders and borrowers...practically no inspection or supervision of bank portfolios existed.... One may conjecture, however, that most depositors felt fully insured and foreign lenders felt that their loans to the private sector were guaranteed by the State.

The two panels of figure 1.6, which plot the public debt/GDP ratios (top panel) and total gross external (public and private) debt (bottom panel) for Iceland and Ireland, faithfully mimic the pattern described by Diaz-Alejandro of "apparent" sound fiscal finances at the outset of the financial crisis.[11] The most onerous sign of future sovereign debt difficulties is shown in the bottom panel of figure 1.6, which highlights the scale of the buildup in mostly private external debts that carried implicit (or explicit) government guarantees.

After more than three years since the onset of the crisis, banking sectors remain riddled with high debts (of which a sizable share are nonperforming) and low levels of capitalization, while the household sector has significant exposures to a depressed real estate market. Under such conditions, the migration of private debts to the public sector and central bank balance sheets is likely to continue, especially in the prevalent environment of indiscriminate, massive bailouts.

Banking Crises as Predictors of Sovereign Debt Problems

Banking crises most often either precede or coincide with sovereign debt crises. The reasons for this temporal sequence may be the contingent liability story emphasized by Diaz-Alejandro (1985) and formalized in Velasco (1987), in which the government takes on massive debts from the private banks, thus undermining its own solvency.[12] The currency crashes that are an integral part of the "twin crisis" phenomenon documented by Kaminsky and Reinhart (1999) would also be consistent with this temporal pattern. If, as they suggest, banking crises precede currency crashes, the collapsing value of the domestic

---

11. We would note that Iceland and Ireland (and also Spain), so often in the news for their present debt difficulties, were exemplary cases of successful public debt reduction up until the eve of the current crisis.

12. See Arellano and Kocherlakota (2008) for a framework that is consistent with these dynamics.

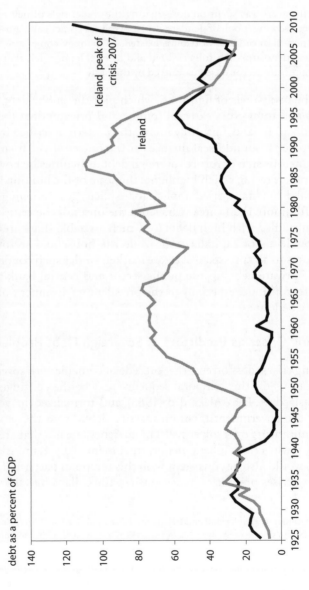

Figure 1.6   Iceland and Ireland: Public debt/GDP and external debt

a. General government (domestic plus external) debt, 1925–2010

debt as a percent of GDP

Iceland peak of crisis, 2007

Ireland

b. External (public plus private) debt, 1970–2010

debt as a percent of GDP

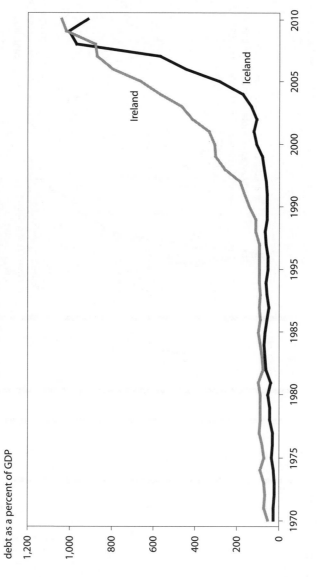

Source: Chapter 2.

Figure 1.7   Sovereign default on external debt, total (domestic plus external) public debt, and systemic banking crises: Advanced economies, 1880–2010

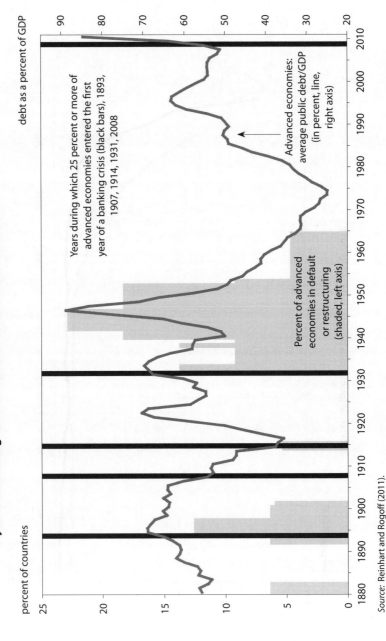

Source: Reinhart and Rogoff (2011).

Table 1.2 Public debt and sovereign default and restructuring: Advanced economies, 1880–2009

Dependent variable	Advanced economies: Share of countries in default or restructuring	
Sample	**1880–2009**	
Independent variables	**OLS (robust errors)**	**Logit (robust errors)**
Advanced economies		
Public debt/GDP (t-1)	*0.209*	*0.002*
p-value	*0*	*0*
Number of observations	130	130
R²	0.176	0.167

Dependent variable	Advanced economies: Share of countries in systemic banking crises	
Sample	**1880–2009**	
Independent variables	**OLS (robust errors)**	**Logit (robust errors)**
Advanced economies		
Public debt/GDP (t-1)	*0.057*	*0.002*
p-value	*0.002*	*0.006*
Number of observations	130	130
R²	0.047	0.05

OLS = ordinary least squares
Logit = logistic regression

Notes: The debt aggregates for the advanced economies and the world are simple arithmetic averages (not weighted by a country's share in world GDP) of individual countries' debt/GDP ratios. For a few countries the time series on debt and exports are much longer dating back to the first half of the 19th century than for nominal GDP. In these cases (Brazil, Canada, Egypt, India, Nicaragua, Thailand, Turkey, and Uruguay) the debt/GDP series was spliced (with appropriate scaling) with the available debt/GDP data. The split between advanced and emerging economies is made along the present-day IMF classification, even though several countries, such as New Zealand, were "emerging markets" during most of the pre-World War I period.

Sources: Chapter 2; Reinhart and Rogoff (2011b), sources cited therein; and authors' calculations.

currency that comes after the banking crisis begins may undermine the solvency of both private and sovereign borrowers who are unfortunate enough to have important amounts of foreign-currency debts. As figure 1.7 and table 1.2 highlight, this is not exclusively an "emerging-market issue," as a higher incidence of sovereign default has followed the major financial crises.

Even absent large-scale bailouts (and without counting postcrisis new government guarantees), we show that largely owing to collapsing revenues, government debts typically rise about 86 percent in the three years following a systemic financial crisis, setting the stage for rating downgrades and, in the worst scenario, default.

A causal chain from sovereign debt crisis to banking crisis, perhaps obscured in these simple graphs, cannot be dismissed lightly. Financial repression and international capital controls may give the government scope to coerce otherwise healthy banks to buy government debt in significant quantities. A government default, in those circumstances, would directly impact the banks' balance sheets. The two crises may be more or less simultaneous. But even if banks are not overly exposed to government paper, the "sovereign ceiling" in which corporate borrowers are rated no higher than their national governments may make banks' offshore borrowing very costly or altogether impossible. The result would be a sudden stop that could give rise to bank insolvencies either immediately or subsequently.

Common Fundamentals, Contagion, or Both?

In this subsection, we emphasize the fundamental distinction between international transmission that occurs due to common shocks (e.g., the collapse of the technology boom in 2001 or the collapse of housing prices in the crisis of the late 2000s) to transmission that occurs primarily due to mechanisms that are really the result of cross-border contagion emanating from the epicenter of the crisis. We offer a rationale for understanding which factors make it more likely that a primarily domestic crisis fuels *fast and furious contagion* (see box 1.2). We use these concepts to discuss the basis for contagion scenarios in Europe and elsewhere. The bunching of banking crises and sovereign debt difficulties across countries is so striking in the late-2000s crisis, where both common shocks and cross-country linkages are evident.

As we discussed in Reinhart and Rogoff (2009), the conjuncture of elements related to the current crisis is illustrative of the two channels of contagion: cross-linkages and common shocks. Without doubt, the US financial crisis of 2007 spilled over into other markets through direct linkages. For example, German and Japanese financial institutions (and others ranging as far as Kazakhstan) sought more attractive returns in the US subprime market, perhaps owing to the fact that profit opportunities in domestic real estate were limited at best and dismal at worst. Indeed, after the fact, it became evident that many financial institutions outside the United States had nontrivial exposure to the US subprime market.[13] This is a classic channel of transmission or contagion through which a crisis in one country spreads across international borders. In the present context, however, contagion or spillovers are only part of the story.

The global nature of the crisis also owes significantly to the fact that many of the features that characterized the run-up to the subprime crisis in the United States were present in many other advanced economies as well. Two common elements stand out. First, many countries in Europe and elsewhere

---

13. Owing to the opaqueness of balance sheets in many financial institutions in these countries, the full extent of exposure is, as yet, unknown.

Box 1.2   Contagion concepts

In defining contagion here, we follow Kaminsky, Reinhart, and Vegh (2003), who distinguish between two types: (1) the "slow-burn" spillover and (2) the kind of fast burn marked by rapid cross-border transmission that Kaminsky, Reinhart, and Vegh label "fast and furious."

We refer to contagion as an episode in which there are significant immediate effects in a number of countries following an event—that is, when the consequences are fast and furious and evolve over a matter of hours or days. This "fast and furious" reaction is a contrast to cases in which the initial international reaction to the news is muted. The latter cases do not preclude the emergence of gradual and protracted effects that may cumulatively have major economic consequences. We refer to these gradual cases as spillovers. Common external shocks, such as changes in international interest rates or oil prices, are also not automatically included in our working definition of contagion. We add to this classification that common shocks need not all be external. This caveat is particularly important with regard to the current episode. Countries may share common "domestic" macroeconomic fundamentals, such as the bursting of a housing bubble, capital inflow bonanzas, increasing private and (or) public leveraging, and so on.

The three pillars of fast and furious contagion are:

1. **Surprise crises and anticipated catastrophes:** Fast and furious crises and contagion cases have a high degree of surprise associated with them, while their quieter counterparts are more broadly anticipated.

2. **Capital flow cycle and leverage:** Fast and furious contagion episodes are typically preceded by a surge in capital inflows and rapidly rising leverage, which come to an abrupt halt or sudden stop in the wake of a crisis. The inflow of capital may come from banks, other financial institutions, or bondholders. The debt contracts typically have short maturities (i.e., investors and financial institutions will have to make decisions about rolling over their debts or not doing so.) With fast and furious contagion, investors and financial institutions that are often highly leveraged are exposed to the crisis country. Such investors can be viewed as halfway through the door, ready to back out on short notice.

3. **Common creditors:** The previous distinction appears to be critical when "potentially affected countries" have a common lender. If the common lender is surprised by the shock in the initial crisis country, there is no time ahead of the impending crisis to rebalance portfolios and scale back from the affected country. In contrast, if the crisis is anticipated, investors have time to limit the damage by scaling back exposure or hedging their positions.

had their own home-grown real estate bubbles (Reinhart and Rogoff 2009). Second, The United States was not alone in running large current account deficits and experiencing a sustained "capital flow bonanza." Bulgaria, Iceland, Ireland, Latvia, New Zealand, Spain, and the United Kingdom, among others, were importing capital from abroad, which helped fuel a credit and asset price boom (Reinhart and Reinhart 2009). These trends, in and of themselves, made these countries vulnerable to the usual nasty consequences of asset market crashes and capital flow reversals irrespective of what may be happening in the United States.

Are more fast and furious episodes or spillovers under way? Applying the criteria that typically characterize fast and furious contagion (see box 1.2) to the current environment yields a mixed picture but one that, on the whole, would suggest contagion (and the more gradual spillover) threats still loom large. Surprise events are (by definition) always a distinct possibility. However, at the time of this writing the precarious nature of balance sheets in much of Europe and the United States is more in the public eye than at the beginning on this crisis in the summer of 2007. This fact is plainly evident in the succession of ratings downgrades of several sovereigns in Europe as well as of Japan. Most recently, of course, Standard and Poor's has put the United States on notice of a possible downgrade, echoing a similar warning by the International Monetary Fund. These sovereign downgrades have mirrored, to some extent, the general widening and greater heterogeneity in sovereign spreads. As to the capital inflow cycle and leverage, the inflow peaks and surges in fresh private borrowing are well behind us but public debts continue to climb (see figure 1.1) and private deleveraging, especially in Europe, has been (at best) limited (Reinhart and Reinhart 2011b). Highly leveraged public and private sectors have been historically a "contagion amplifier." So have been common creditors. Apart from the elevated levels of leverage in most advanced economies as discussed, the widespread presence of common creditors (most notable in the euro area as well as the United Kingdom) is a second compelling factor indicating that the scope for fast and furious contagion remains high. This type of financial vulnerability is exacerbated by the lack of transparency in overall cross-border exposure, as highlighted in the extensive new database in Milesi-Ferretti, Strobbe, and Tamirisa (2010).

IV. Debt and Growth

The march from high public indebtedness to sovereign default or restructuring is usually marked by episodes of drama, punctuated by periods of high volatility in financial markets, rising credit spreads, and ratings downgrades. However, the economic impacts of high public indebtedness are not limited to such episodes of high drama, as rising public debts are not universally associated with rising interest rates and imminent expectations of sovereign default (see Gagnon and Hinterschweiger 2011 for a thorough examination of this issue.) Serious public debt overhangs may also cast a shadow on economic growth, even when the sovereign's solvency is not called into question.

In this section we summarize our main findings in Reinhart and Rogoff (2010a, 2010b), elaborate on some methodology issues, and discuss some of the very recent literature that examines the debt and growth connection.

The Basic Exercise and Key Results

Our analysis of growth and debt was based on newly compiled data on 44 countries spanning about 200 years. This amounts to 3,700 annual observations and covers a wide range of political systems, institutions, exchange rate arrangements, and historic circumstances.

The main findings of Reinhart and Rogoff (2010a) are the following.

- First, the relationship between government debt and real GDP growth is weak for debt/GDP ratios below 90 percent of GDP.[14] Above the threshold of 90 percent, median growth rates fall by 1 percent, and average growth falls considerably more. The threshold for public debt is similar in advanced and emerging-market economies and applies for both the post–World War II period and as far back as the data permit (often well into the 1800s).

- Second, emerging markets face lower thresholds for total external debt (public and private)—which is usually denominated in a foreign currency. When total external debt reaches 60 percent of GDP, annual growth declines about 2 percent; for higher levels, growth rates are roughly cut in half.

- Third, there is no apparent contemporaneous link between inflation and public debt levels for the advanced countries as a group (some countries, such as the United States, have experienced higher inflation when debt/GDP is high). The story is entirely different for emerging markets, where inflation rises sharply as debt increases.

Figure 1.8 can be used to summarize our main conclusions. The top panel applies to the 20 advanced countries in our 44-country sample (where much of the public debate is centered).[15] The remaining two panels of the figure present comparable results for emerging-market public debt and gross external debt.

---

14. As noted previously, "public debt" here refers to gross central government debt. "Domestic public debt" is government debt issued under domestic legal jurisdiction. Public debt does not include obligations carrying a government guarantee. Total gross external debt includes the external debts of *all* branches of government as well as private debt issued by domestic private entities under a foreign jurisdiction.

15. The comparable emerging-market exercises are presented in the original working paper (NBER Working Paper 15639, January 2010).

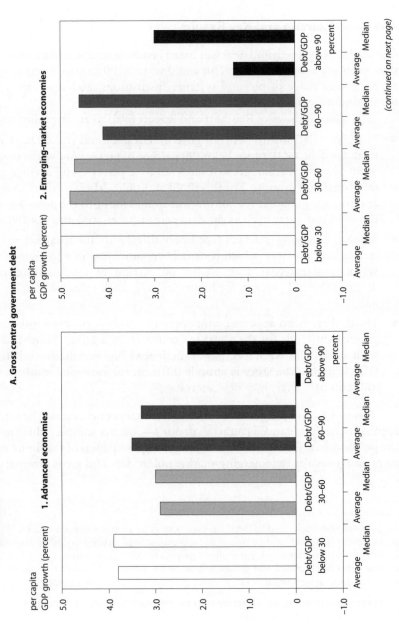

Figure 1.8 Debt and real per capita GDP growth: Selected advanced and emerging-market economies, 1946–2009

A. Gross central government debt

1. Advanced economies

2. Emerging-market economies

per capita GDP growth (percent)

(continued on next page)

B. Gross external (public plus private) debt

per capita
GDP growth (percent)   **1. Emerging-market economies**

Sources: Reinhart and Rogoff (2010a) and sources cited therein.

In the figure, the annual observations are grouped into four categories, according to the ratio of debt/GDP during that particular year: years when debt-to-GDP levels were below 30 percent; 30 to 60 percent; 60 to 90 percent; and above 90 percent.[16] The bars show average and median GDP growth for each of the four debt categories. Note that of the 1,186 annual observations, there are a significant number in each category, including 96 above 90 percent. (Recent observations in that top bracket come from Belgium, Greece, Italy, and Japan.) From the figure, it is evident that there is no obvious link between debt and growth until public debt exceeds the 90 percent threshold. The observations with debt to GDP over 90 percent have median growth roughly 1 percent lower than the lower debt burden groups and mean levels of growth almost 4 percent lower. (Using lagged debt does not dramatically change the picture.)

---

16. The four "buckets" encompassing low, medium-low, medium-high, and high debt levels are based on our interpretation of much of the literature and policy discussion on what are considered low, high debt levels. It parallels the World Bank country groupings according to four income groups. Sensitivity analysis involving a different set of debt cutoffs merits exploration, as do country-specific debt thresholds along the broad lines discussed in Reinhart, Rogoff, and Savastano (2003).

Table 1.3 Real GDP growth as the level of government debt varies: Selected advanced economies, 1790–2009 (annual percent change)

Country	Period	Central (federal) government debt/GDP			
		Below 30 percent	30 to 60 percent	60 to 90 percent	90 percent and above
Australia	1902–2009	3.1	4.1	2.3	4.6
Austria	1880–2009	4.3	3.0	2.3	n.a.
Belgium	1835–2009	3.0	2.6	2.1	3.3
Canada	1925–2009	2.0	4.5	3.0	2.2
Denmark	1880–2009	3.1	1.7	2.4	n.a.
Finland	1913–2009	3.2	3.0	4.3	1.9
France	1880–2009	4.9	2.7	2.8	2.3
Germany	1880–2009	3.6	0.9	n.a.	n.a.
Greece	1884–2009	4.0	*0.3*	*4.8*	2.5
Ireland	1949–2009	4.4	4.5	4.0	2.4
Italy	1880–2009	*5.4*	*4.9*	1.9	0.7
Japan	1885–2009	4.9	3.7	3.9	0.7
Netherlands	1880–2009	4.0	2.8	2.4	2.0
New Zealand	1932–2009	2.5	2.9	3.9	*3.6*
Norway	1880–2009	2.9	4.4	n.a.	n.a.
Portugal	1851–2009	4.8	2.5	1.4	n.a.
Spain	1850–2009	*1.6*	3.3	*1.3*	2.2
Sweden	1880–2009	2.9	2.9	2.7	n.a.
United Kingdom	1830–2009	2.5	2.2	2.1	1.8
United States	1790–2009	4.0	3.4	3.3	*−1.8*
Average		**3.7**	**3.0**	**3.4**	**1.7**
Median		**3.9**	**3.1**	**2.8**	**1.9**
Number of observations = **2,317**		866	654	445	352

Notes: n.a. denotes no observations were recorded for that particular debt range. There are missing observations, most notably during World War I and II years; further details are provided in the data appendices to Reinhart and Rogoff (2009) and are available from the authors. Minimum and maximum values for each debt range are shown in **bold italics**.

Sources: There are many sources; among the more prominent are International Monetary Fund, *World Economic Outlook*; OECD; World Bank, *Global Development Finance*. Extensive other sources are cited in Reinhart and Rogoff (2009).

High Debt Episodes in the Sample

The episodes that attract our interest are those where debt levels were historically high. As convenient as it is to focus exclusively on a particular country or a single episode for a single country (like the United States around World War II, where the data are readily available, or an interesting ongoing case like Japan), the basis for an empirical regularity is multiple observations. Because our data span 44 countries with many going back to the 1800s or at least the beginning of the 19th century, our analysis is based on all the episodes of high (above 90 percent) debt for the post–World War II period; for the pre-war sample it covers all those for which data are available. Table 1.3 is reproduced from Reinhart and Rogoff (2010a) and describes the coverage and the basic statistics for the various debt levels for the advanced economies.[17]

It is common knowledge that the United States emerged after World War II with a very high debt level. But this also held for Australia, Canada, and most markedly the United Kingdom, where public debt/GDP peaked at near 240 percent in 1948. These cases from the aftermath of World War II are joined in our sample by a number of peacetime high-debt episodes: the 1920s and 1980s to the present in Belgium; the 1920s in France; Greece in the 1920s, 1930s, and 1990s to the present; Ireland in the 1980s; Italy in the 1990s; Spain at the turn of the last century; the United Kingdom in the interwar period and prior to the 1860s; and, of course, Japan in the past decade. As will be discussed, episodes where debt is above 90 percent are themselves rare, and as shown in table 1.3, a number of countries have never had debt entries above 90 percent.

Debt Thresholds and Nonlinearities: The 90 Percent Benchmark

Thresholds and nonlinearities play a key role in understanding the relationship between debt and growth that should not be ignored in casual reinterpretations.

Thresholds. Anyone who has done any work with data is well aware that mapping a vague concept, such as "high debt" or "overvalued" exchange rates to a workable definition for interpreting the existing facts and informing the discussion requires making arbitrary judgments about where to draw lines. In the case of debt, we worked with four buckets: 0 to 30 percent, 30 to 60 percent, 60 to 90 percent, and over 90 percent. The last one turned out to be the critical one for detecting a difference in growth performance, so we single it out for discussion here.

Figure 1.9 shows the public debt to GDP ratio as well as pooled descriptive statistics (inset) for the advanced economies (to complement the country-specific ones shown in table 1.3) over the post World War II period.[18] The median public debt/GDP ratio is 36.4 percent; about 92 percent of the observations fall below the 90 percent threshold (see figure 1.9). In effect, about 76 percent of the observations were below the 60 percent Maastricht criteria.

---

17. Again, the interested reader is referred to the original working paper version of Reinhart and Rogoff (2010a). See NBER Working Paper 15639 (January 2010).

18. Our sample includes 24 emerging-market countries.

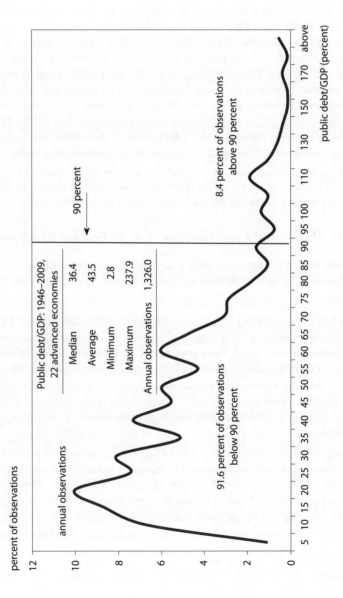

Figure 1.9   The 90 percent debt/GDP threshold: 1946–2009, advanced economies probability density function

percent of observations

Public debt/GDP: 1946–2009, 22 advanced economies	
Median	36.4
Average	43.5
Minimum	2.8
Maximum	237.9
Annual observations	1,326.0

annual observations

90 percent

8.4 percent of observations above 90 percent

91.6 percent of observations below 90 percent

public debt/GDP (percent)

Notes: The advanced economy sample is the complete IMF grouping (Switzerland and Iceland were added). It includes Australia, Austria, Belgium, Canada, Denmark, Finland, France, Germany, Greece, Iceland, Ireland, Italy, Japan, Netherlands, New Zealand, Norway, Portugal, Spain, Sweden, Switzerland, the United Kingdom, and the United States.

Put differently, our "high vulnerability" region for lower growth (the area under the curve to the right of the 90 percent line) comprises only about 8 percent of the sample population. The standard considerations about type I and type II errors apply here.[19] If we raise the upper bucket cutoff much above 90 percent, then we are relegating the high-debt analysis to case studies (the United Kingdom in 1946–50 and Japan in recent years). Only about 2 percent of the observations are at debt-to-GDP levels at or above 120 percent, and that includes the aforementioned cases.

If debt levels above 90 percent are indeed as benign as some suggest, one might have expected to see a higher incidence of these over the long course of history. Certainly our read of the evidence, as underscored by the central theme of our 2009 book This Time Is Different: Eight Centuries of Financial Folly, hardly suggests that politicians are universally too cautious in accumulating high debt levels. Quite the contrary, far too often they take undue risks with debt buildups, relying implicitly perhaps on the fact that these risks often take a very long time to materialize. If debt-to-GDP levels over 90 percent are so benign, then generations of politicians must have been overlooking proverbial money on the street.

We do not pretend to argue that growth will be normal at 89 percent and subpar (about 1 percent lower) at 91 percent debt/GDP any more than a car crash is unlikely at 54 miles per hour and near certain at 56 miles per hour. However, mapping the theoretical notion of *vulnerability regions* to bad outcomes by necessity involves defining thresholds, just as traffic signs in the United States specify speed of 55 miles per hour.[20]

Nonlinear relationship. In Reinhart and Rogoff (2010a), we summarized our results thus:

> ...the relationship between government debt and real GDP growth is weak for debt/GDP ratios below a threshold of 90 percent of GDP. Above 90 percent, median growth rates fall by one percent, and average growth falls considerably more.

Revisiting figure 1.8 is useful for illustrating the importance of nonlinearities in the debt-growth link. Simply put, for 92 percent of the observations in our sample there is no systematic link between debt and growth.[21] Thus, if one were to do a simple scatterplot of all the observations on debt/GDP and on growth one would expect to find a "clouded mess." We can highlight this general point with the US case. As we noted in the working paper version of Reinhart and Rogoff (2010a), for the period 1790–2009, there are a total of 216 observations of which 211 (or 98 percent) are below the 90 percent debt-to-

---

19. The null hypothesis is whatever "normal" growth is versus the alternative of lower growth.

20. These methodology issues are discussed in Kaminsky and Reinhart (1999).

21. Bruno and Easterly (1998) find similar nonlinearities in the inflation-growth relationship.

GDP cutoff. It should be quite obvious that a scatterplot of the US data would not be capable of revealing a systematic pattern (as demonstrated in Iron and Bivens 2010). Indeed, this example illustrates one of our main results: that there is no systematic relationship between debt and growth below a threshold of 90 percent of GDP.

Debt and Growth Causality

As discussed, we examine average and median growth and inflation rates contemporaneously with debt. Temporal causality tests are not part of the analysis. The application of many of the standard methods for establishing temporal precedence is complicated by the nonlinear relationship between growth and debt (more of this to follow) that we have alluded to.

But where do we place the evidence on causality? For low-to-moderate levels of debt there may or may not be one; the issue is an empirical one, which merits study. For high levels of debt the evidence points to bi-directional causality.

Growth-to-debt: As we discuss in section II, our analysis of the aftermath of financial crisis (Reinhart and Rogoff 2008) presents compelling evidence for both advanced and emerging markets over 1800–2008 on the fiscal impacts (revenue, deficits, debts, and sovereign credit ratings) of the recessions associated with banking crises (figure 1.2).

There is little room to doubt that severe economic downturns, irrespective of whether their origins was a financial crisis or not, will, in most instances, lead to higher debt/GDP levels contemporaneously and/or with a lag. There is, of course, a vast literature on cyclically adjusted fiscal deficits making exactly this point.

Debt-to-growth: A unilateral causal pattern from growth to debt, however, does not accord with the evidence. Public debt surges are associated with a higher incidence of debt crises (figure 1.4).[22] This temporal pattern is analyzed in Reinhart and Rogoff (2008) and in the accompanying country-by-country analyses cited therein (Reinhart and Rogoff 2011b). In the current context, even a cursory reading of the recent turmoil in Greece and other European countries can be importantly traced to the adverse impacts of high levels of government debt (or potentially guaranteed debt) on country risk and economic outcomes. At a very basic level, a high public debt burden implies higher future taxes (inflation is also a tax) or lower future government spending, if the government is expected to repay its debts.

There is scant evidence to suggest that high debt has little impact on growth. Kumar and Woo (2010) highlight in their cross-country findings that debt levels

---

22. For a model where credit-financed government deficits lead to a currency crisis, see Krugman (1979).

have negative consequences for subsequent growth, even after controlling for other standard determinants in growth equations. For emerging markets, an older literature on the debt overhang of the 1980s frequently addresses this theme.

V. The Aftermath of High Debt: The 1930s and World War II

Up until very recently, financial markets and policymakers had all but forgotten that default and restructuring are not alien to the advanced economies. For instance, Reinhart, Rogoff, and Savastano (2003) and Reinhart and Rogoff (2009) document that several now-wealthy countries have a long history of serial default. This section does not attempt to review this rich sovereign debt crisis history; the focus is confined to the last two "global" debt spikes. These two high-debt episodes share some of the characteristics of the current debt spike, as they involve numerous advanced economies (accounting for an important share of world GDP).

The first part of the section presents a brief sketch of the last wave of sovereign defaults, restructurings, and forcible conversions in response to the debt overhang during the 1930s that engulfed the advanced economies while the second subsection outlines the more subtle debt restructuring that was facilitated by pervasive financial repression during the 1940s to the 1970s.

Default, Restructurings, and Forcible Conversions in the 1930s

Table 1.4 lists the known "domestic credit events" of the Great Depression. Default on or restructuring of external debt (see the notes to the table) also often accompanied the restructuring or default of the domestic debt. All the allied governments, with the exception of Finland, defaulted on (and remained in default through 1939 and never repaid) their World War I debts to the United States as economic conditions deteriorated worldwide during the 1930s.[23]

Financial Repression in 1940s–70s: The "Quiet" Restructuring

Apart from emerging markets, many of which have continued to openly periodically default or restructure their debts (usually at times of severe economic stress) through the present, the only explicit defaults (or restructurings) in advanced economies since World War II were confined to either those of the countries that lost the war (Austria, Germany, Italy, and Japan) or those that never reestablished their credit since slipping into default in the 1930s (Greece, for instance, was in default from 1932 until 1964). Financial repression was the post-World War II "politically correct" replacement for the more open debt restructurings and defaults of the 1930s.

---

23. Finland, being under continuous threat of Soviet invasion at the time, maintained payments on its debts to the United States so as to maintain the best possible relationship.

Table 1.4 Selected episodes of domestic debt default or restructuring, 1920s–40s

Country	Dates	Commentary
For additional possible domestic defaults in several European countries during the 1930s, see notes below.		
Australia	1931/1932	The Debt Conversion Agreement Act in 1931/32 appears to have done something similar to the later New Zealand induced conversion. See New Zealand entry.[1]
Bolivia	1927	Arrears of interest lasted until at least 1940.
Canada (Alberta)	April 1935	The only province to default—which lasted for about 10 years.
China	1932	First of several "consolidations", monthly cost of domestic service was cut in half. Interest rates were reduced to 6 percent (from over 9 percent)—amortization periods were about doubled in length.
Greece	1932	Interest on domestic debt was reduced by 75 percent since 1932; domestic debt was about 1/4 of total public debt.
Mexico	1930s	Service on external debt was suspended in 1928. During the 1930s, interest payments included "arrears of expenditure and civil and military pensions."
New Zealand	1933	In March 1933 the New Zealand Debt Conversion Act was passed providing for voluntary conversion of internal debt amounting to 113 million pounds to an interest rate of 4 percent for ordinary debt and 3 percent for tax-free debt. Holders had the option of dissenting but interest in the dissented portion was made subject to an interest tax of 33.3 percent.[1]
Peru	1931	After suspending service on external debt on May 29, Peru made "partial interest payments" on domestic debt.
Romania	February 1933	Redemption of domestic and foreign debt is suspended (except for three loans).
Spain	October 1936–April 1939	Interest payments on external debt were suspended; arrears on domestic debt service accumulated.
United States	1933	Abrogation of the gold clause. In effect, the US refused to pay Panama the annuity in gold due to Panama according to a 1903 treaty. The dispute was settled in 1936 when the US paid the agreed amount in gold *balboas*.
United Kingdom	1932	Most of the outstanding World War I debt was consolidated into a 3.5 percent perpetual annuity. This domestic debt conversion was apparently voluntary. However, some of the World War I debts to the United States were issued under domestic (UK) law (and therefore classified as domestic debt) and these were defaulted on following the end of the Hoover 1931 moratorium.

(continued on next page)

Table 1.4   Selected episodes of domestic debt default or restructuring, 1920s–40s *(continued)*

Uruguay	November 1, 1932–February, 1937	After suspending redemption of external debt on January 20, redemptions on domestic debt were equally suspended.
Austria	December 1945	Restoration of schilling (150 limit per person); remainder placed in blocked accounts. In December 1947, large amounts of previously blocked schillings were invalidated and rendered worthless; temporary blockage of 50 percent of deposits.
Germany	June 20, 1948	Monetary reform limiting 40 deutsche mark per person; partial cancellation and blocking of all accounts.
Japan	March 2, 1946–1952	After inflation, exchange of all bank notes for new issue (1 to 1) limited to 100 yen per person; remaining balances were deposited in blocked accounts.
Russia	1947	The monetary reform subjected privately held currency to a 90 percent reduction.
	April 10, 1957	Repudiation of domestic debt (about 253 billion rubles at the time).

1. See Schedvin (1970) and Prichard (1970), for accounts of the Australian and New Zealand conversions, respectively, during the Depression. Michael Reddell kindly alerted us to these episodes and references.

Notes: We have made significant further progress in sorting out the defaults on World War I debts to the United States, notably by European countries. In all cases these episodes are classified as a default on external debts. However, in some cases—such as the United Kingdom—some of the World War I debts to the United States were also issued under domestic law and, as such, would also qualify as a domestic default. The external defaults on June 15, 1934 included Austria, Belgium, Czechoslovakia, Estonia, France, Greece, Hungary, Italy, Latvia, Poland, the United Kingdom. Only Finland made payments. See *New York Times*, June 15, 1934.

Generally, the aims of debt restructuring are (1) reducing the value of the stock of existing debts (haircut); (2) reducing debt servicing costs (by cutting or capping interest rates); and (3) minimizing rollover risk by lengthening maturities and/or shifting into nonmarketable debt. Financial repression achieves all three goals of debt restructuring—albeit that the first (reducing the value) is achieved more gradually than in open restructurings. Thus, as argued in Reinhart and Rogoff (2009), financial repression—a hallmark of the 1940s–70s—is nothing other than a more subtle form of debt restructuring.

Legislation or "moral suasion" limiting the range and amounts of nongovernment debt domestic assets financial institutions can hold; limiting further (or outright forbidding) holdings of foreign assets; and requiring financial institutions to hold more government debt were all part of the "financially repressed landscape." A whole range of interest rate ceilings (for example, on deposits) made holding low-yielding government bonds also more palatable for individuals as well as institutions. Pension funds have historically provided the "captive audience par excellence" for placing vast sums of government debt at questionable rates of return (often negative ex post in real terms). It is worth noting that the real ex post interest rate on public debt (appropriately weighted

Table 1.5 Debt liquidation through financial repression: Italy, United Kingdom, and United States, 1945–55

Country	Public debt/GDP			Annual average: 1946–1955	
	1945	1955 (actual)	1955 without repression savings (estimate)[3]	"Financial repression revenue"/ GDP	Inflation
Italy[1]	79.2	38.1	129.3	9.1	10.8
United Kingdom[2]	215.6	138.2	182.9	4.5	5.9
United States	116.0	66.2	118.6	5.2	4.2

1. Italy was in default on its external debt 1940–46.
2. The savings from financial repression are a lower bound, as we use the "official" consumer price index for this period in the calculations and inflation is estimated to have been substantially higher than the official figure (see for example Friedman and Schwartz 1963).
3. The simple cumulative annual savings without compounding.

Notes: The peaks in debt/GDP were: Italy 129.0 in 1943; United Kingdom 247.5 in 1946; United States 121.3 in 1946. An alternative interpretation of the financial repression revenue is simply as savings in interest service on the debt.

Source: Reinhart and Sbrancia (2011).

by the type of debt instrument) was negative for US debt for 25 percent of the years during 1945–80, while the comparable share for the United Kingdom was nearly 50 percent, as Reinhart and Sbrancia (2011) document.

Table 1.5 illustrates, for the examples of Italy, the United Kingdom, and the United States, the important role played by financial repression (combined with some inflation) in the crucial debt-reduction decade that followed World War II.[24] The savings range from an average of about 9 percent for Italy (which had higher inflation) to about 5 percent for the United States and United Kingdom. In effect, the savings from financial repression are a lower bound for the United Kingdom, as we use the "official" consumer price index for this period in the calculations and inflation is estimated to have been substantially higher than the official figure (see, for example, Friedman and Schwartz 1963). Also, other factors (such as the 1951 US conversion, which swapped marketable for nonmarketable debt) do not factor into these simple debt-reduction calculations. The simple fact is that ex post real interest rates were significantly lower in both advanced and emerging-market economies during the financial repression era that is sandwiched between World War II and the high real interest rates of the 1930s and the post-financial and capital account liberalization that has swept through financial markets since the mid-1980s.

---

24. See Reinhart and Sbrancia (2011) for a full fledged analysis of the international role played by financial repression in reducing the World War II debt overhang.

VI. Conclusion

One need look no further than the stubbornly high unemployment rates in the United States and other advanced economies to be convinced of the importance of developing a better understanding of the growth prospects for the decade ahead. We have presented evidence suggesting that high levels of debt dampen growth. One can argue that the United States can tolerate higher levels of debt more than other countries can without having its solvency called into question. That is probably so.[25] We have shown in our earlier work that a country's credit history plays a prominent role in determining what levels of debt it can sustain without landing on a sovereign debt crisis. More to the point of this analysis, however, we have no comparable evidence yet to suggest that the consequences of higher debt levels for growth will be different for the United States than for other advanced economies.

Figure 1.10, which plots total (public and private) credit market debt outstanding for the United States during 1916 to 2010Q1, makes this point clear.[26] Despite considerable deleveraging by the private financial sector, total debt remains near its historic high in 2008. Total public-sector debt during the first quarter of 2010 is 117 percent of GDP; since 1916 (when this series begins) it has been higher only during a one-year stint at 119 percent in 1945. Perhaps soaring US debt levels will not prove to be a drag on growth in the decades to come. However, if history is any guide, that is a risky proposition, and overreliance on US exceptionalism may only prove to be one more example of the This Time is Different Syndrome.[27]

The sharp runup in public-sector debt will likely prove one of the most enduring legacies of the 2007–09 financial crises in the United States and elsewhere. We examine the experience of 44 countries spanning up to two centuries of data on central government debt, inflation, and growth. Our main finding is that across both advanced countries and emerging markets, high debt/GDP levels (90 percent and above) are associated with notably lower-growth outcomes. Much lower levels of external debt/GDP (60 percent) are associated with adverse outcomes for emerging-market growth. Seldom do countries "grow" their way out of debts. The nonlinear response of growth to debt as

---

25. Indeed, this is the central argument in Reinhart and Reinhart (2010), originally published on November 17, 2008.

26. The Flow of Funds data aggregate the private and public sectors, where the latter comprises federal (net), state, and local government enterprises. To reiterate, this is not the public debt measure used in our historical analysis; we use gross central government debt (which for the United States is at present about 90 percent of GDP).

27. The This Time is Different Syndrome is rooted in the firmly held beliefs that (1) financial crises and negative outcomes are something that happen to other people in other countries at other times (these do not happen here and now to us); (2) we are doing things better, we are smarter, we have learned from the past mistakes; and (3) as a consequence, old rules of valuation are not thought to apply any longer.

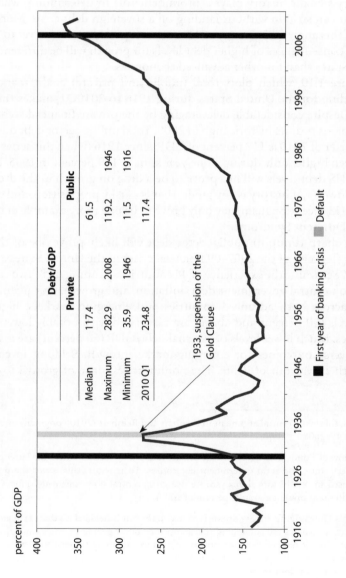

Figure 1.10 Total (public and private) credit market debt outstanding: United States, 1916–2010Q1

percent of GDP

	Debt/GDP			
	Private		Public	
Median	117.4		61.5	
Maximum	282.9	2008	119.2	1946
Minimum	35.9	1946	11.5	1916
2010 Q1	234.8		117.4	

1933, suspension of the Gold Clause

■ First year of banking crisis   ■ Default

Notes: Beginning in 2010 Q1, almost all Fannie Mae and Freddie Mac mortgage pools are consolidated in Fannie Mae's and Freddie Mac's balance sheets and, thus, are included in the debt of government

Source: Chapter 2.

34

debt grows toward historical boundaries is reminiscent of the "debt intolerance" phenomenon developed in Reinhart, Rogoff, and Savastano (2003). As countries hit debt intolerance ceilings, market interest rates can begin to rise quite suddenly, forcing painful adjustment.

For many if not most advanced countries, dismissing debt concerns at this time is tantamount to ignoring the proverbial elephant in the room. So is pretending that no restructuring will be necessary. It may not be called restructuring, so as not to offend the sensitivities of governments that want to pretend to find an advanced-economy solution for an emerging market style sovereign debt crisis. As in other debt crisis resolution episodes, debt buybacks and debt-equity swaps are a part of the restructuring landscape. Financial repression is not likely to also prove a politically correct term—so prudential regulation will probably provide the aegis for a return to a system more akin to what the global economy had prior to the 1980s market-based reforms.

The process where debts are being "placed" at below-market interest rates in pension funds and other more captive domestic financial institutions is already under way in several countries in Europe. Central banks on both sides of the Atlantic have become even bigger players in purchases of government debt, possibly for the indefinite future. For the United States, fear of currency appreciation continues to drive central banks in many emerging markets to purchase US government bonds on a large scale. In other words, markets for government bonds are increasingly populated by nonmarket players, calling into question the information content of bond prices relative to their underlying risk profile—a common feature of financially repressed systems.

References

Arellano, Cristina, and Narayana Kocherlakota. 2008. *Internal Debt Crises and Sovereign Defaults.* NBER Working paper 13794. Cambridge, MA: National Bureau of Economic Research.

Bordo, Michael, and Barry Eichengreen. 1999. *Is Our Current International Economic Environment Unusually Crisis Prone?* Paper prepared for Reserve Bank of Australia conference on private capital, Sydney, August.

Bordo, Michael, Barry Eichengreen, Daniela Klingebiel, and Maria Soledad Martinez-Peria. 2001. Is the Crisis Problem Growing More Severe? *Economic Policy* 16 (April): 51–82.

Bruno, Michael, and William Easterly. 1998. Inflation Crises and Long-Run Growth. *Journal of Monetary Economics* 41, no. 1 (February): 3–26.

Calvo, Guillermo. 1988. Servicing the Public Debt: The Role of Expectations. *American Economic Review* 78, no. 4 (September): 647–61.

Caprio, Gerard, Daniela Klingebiel, Luc Laeven, and Guillermo Noguera. 2005. Banking Crisis Database. In *Systemic Financial Crises*, ed. Patrick Honohan and Luc Laeven. Cambridge: Cambridge University Press.

Checherita, Christina, and Philipp Rother. 2010. *The Impact of High and Growing Debt on Economic Growth and Empirical Investigation for the Euro Area.* European Central Bank Working Paper Series no. 1237 (August). Frankfurt: European Central Bank.

Diaz-Alejandro, Carlos. 1985. Goodbye Financial Repression, Hello Financial Crash. *Journal of Development Economics* 19.

Easterly, William R. 1989. Fiscal Adjustment and Deficit Financing During the Debt Crisis. In *Dealing with the Debt Crisis, ed.* I. Husain and I. Diwan. Washington: World Bank.

Eichengreen, Barry. 1992. *Golden Fetters The Gold Standard and the Great Depression 1919–1939*. New York: Oxford University Press.

Eichengreen, Barry, and Peter H. Lindert, eds. 1989. *The International Debt Crisis in Historical Perspective*. Cambridge, MA: MIT Press.

Flandreau, Marc, and Frederic Zumer. 2004. *The Making of Global Finance, 1880–1913*. Paris: Organization for Economic Cooperation and Development.

Fostel, Ana, and John Geanokoplos. 2008. Leverage Cycles and the Anxious Economy. *American Economic Review* 98, no. 4: 1211–44.

Friedman, Milton, and Anna Jacobson Schwartz. 1963. *A Monetary History of the United States 1867–1960*. Princeton: Princeton University Press.

Gagnon, Joseph, with Marc Hinterschweiger. 2011. *The Global Outlook for Government Debt over the Next 25 Years: Implications for the Economy and Public Policy*. Policy Analyses in International Economics 94. Washington: Peterson Institute for International Economics.

Geanokoplos, John. 2009. The Leverage Cycle. In *NBER Macroeconomic Annual 2009*, volume 24, ed. D. Acemoglu, K. Rogoff and M. Woodford. Chicago: University of Chicago Press.

Giovannini, Alberto, and Martha de Melo. 1993. Government Revenue from Financial Repression. *American Economic Review* 83, no. 4: 953–63.

Gopinath, Gita, and Mark Aguiar. 2006. Defaultable Risk, Interest Rates and the Current Account. *Journal of International Economics* 69, no. 1 (June).

Jeanne, Olivier. 2009. Debt Maturity and the International Financial Architecture. *American Economic Review* 99, no. 5: 2135–48.

Kaminsky, Graciela L., and Carmen M. Reinhart. 1999. The Twin Crises: The Causes of Banking and Balance of Payments Problems. *American Economic Review* 89, no. 3 (June): 473–500.

Kaminsky, Graciela L., Carmen M. Reinhart, and Carlos Vegh. 2003. The Unholy Trinity of Financial Contagion. *Journal of Economic Perspectives* 17, no. 4 (Fall): 51–74.

Krugman, Paul R. 1979. A Model of Balance of Payments Crises. *Journal of Money, Credit and Banking* 11 (August): 311–25.

Kindleberger, Charles P. 1989. *Manias, Panics and Crashes: A History of Financial Crises*. New York: Basic Books.

Lazaretou, Sophia. 2005. Greek Monetary Economics in Retrospect: The Adventures of the Drachma. *Economic Notes by Banca Monte dei Paschi di Siena* 34, no. 3: 331–70.

Kumar, Mohan, and Jaejoon Woo. 2010. *Public Debt and Growth*. IMF Working Paper WP/10/174 (July). Washington: International Monetary Fund.

Lindert, Peter H., and Peter J. Morton. 1989. How Sovereign Debt Has Worked. In *Developing Country Debt and Economic Performance, volume 1,* ed. Jeffrey Sachs. Chicago: University of Chicago Press.

Mendoza, Enrique G., and Marco E. Terrones. 2008. *An Anatomy of Credit Booms: Evidence from Macro Aggregates and Micro Data*. NBER Working Paper 14049 (May). Cambridge, MA: National Bureau of Economic Research.

Milesi-Ferretti, Gian Maria, Francesco Strobbe, and Natalia Tamirisa. 2010. *Bilateral Financial Linkages and Global Imbalances: A View on The Eve of the Financial Crisis*. IMF Working Paper 10/257. Washington: International Monetary Fund.

Obstfeld, Maurice, and Kenneth Rogoff. 1995. *Foundations of International Economics*. Cambridge, MA: MIT Press.

Prichard, Muriel F. Lloyds. 1970. *An Economic History of New Zealand to 1939*. Auckland: Collins.

Reinhart, Carmen M., and Vincent R. Reinhart. 2009. Capital Flow Bonanzas: An Encompassing View of the Past and Present. In *NBER International Seminar in Macroeconomics 2008*, ed. Jeffrey Frankel and Francesco Giavazzi. Chicago: Chicago University Press for National Bureau of Economic Research.

Reinhart, Carmen M., and Vincent R. Reinhart. 2010. *Is the US Too Big to Fail?* VoxEU, May 9, www.voxeu.org. Originally posted November 17, 2008.

Reinhart, Carmen M., and Vincent R. Reinhart. 2011 (forthcoming). After the Fall. Forthcoming in Federal Reserve Bank of Kansas City Economic Policy Symposium, *Macroeconomic Challenges: The Decade Ahead*, Jackson Hole, Wyoming, August 26-28, 2010.

Reinhart, Carmen M., and Kenneth S. Rogoff. 2004. The Modern History of Exchange Rate Arrangements: A Reinterpretation. *Quarterly Journal of Economics* CXIX, no. 1 (February): 1–48.

Reinhart, Carmen M., and Kenneth S. Rogoff. 2008. *This Time is Different: A Panoramic View of Eight Centuries of Financial Crises*. NBER Working Paper 13882 (March). Cambridge, MA: National Bureau of Economic Research.

Reinhart, Carmen M., and Kenneth S Rogoff. 2009. *This Time is Different: Eight Centuries of Financial Folly*. Princeton: Princeton University Press (October).

Reinhart, Carmen M., and Kenneth S. Rogoff. 2010a. Growth in a Time of Debt. *American Economic Review* 100, no. 2 (May): 573–78. Also published as NBER Working Paper 15639 (January 2010).

Reinhart, Carmen M., and Kenneth S. Rogoff. 2010b. *Debt and Growth Revisited*. VoxEU, August 11, www.voxeu.org.

Reinhart, Carmen M., and Kenneth S. Rogoff. 2011a (forthcoming). Domestic Debt: The Forgotten History. *Economic Journal* (May).

Reinhart, Carmen M., and Kenneth S Rogoff. 2011b (forthcoming). From Financial Crash to Debt Crisis. *American Economic Review*. Also published as NBER Working Paper 15795 (March 2010).

Reinhart, Carmen M., and M. Belen Sbrancia. 2011. *The Liquidation of Government Debt*. Working Paper 11-10. Washington: Peterson Institute for International Economics.

Reinhart, Carmen M., Kenneth S. Rogoff, and Miguel A. Savastano. 2003. Debt Intolerance. *Brookings Papers on Economic Activity* 1 (Spring): 1–74.

Rodrik, Dani, and Andres Velasco. 2000. Short-Term Capital Flows. In *Annual World Bank Conference on Development Economics* (April). Washington: World Bank.

Schedvin, C. B. 1970. *Australia and the Great Depression*. Sydney: Sydney University Press.

Velasco, Andres. 1987. Financial and Balance-of-Payments Crises. *Journal of Development Economics* 27, no. 1/2 (October): 263–83.

Winkler, Max. 1933. *Foreign Bonds: An Autopsy*. Philadelphia: Roland Sway Co.

Wynne, William H. 1951. *State Insolvency and Foreign Bondholders: Selected Case Histories of Governmental Foreign Bond Defaults and Debt Readjustments* II. London: Oxford University Press.

2

Chartbook of Country Histories of Debt, Default, and Financial Crises

CARMEN M. REINHART

I. Preamble

This chartbook provides a pictorial history, on a country-by-country basis, of debt and economic crises of various forms. It systematically illustrates for 70 countries the individual timeline of public and private debts, banking, sovereign domestic and external debt crises, and hyperinflation, starting from a country's independence (and even prior to that in numerous cases) to the present. The dating of the largest output declines and a country's history with International Monetary Fund (IMF) programs since World War II to deal with an assortment of economic ills contribute to the chronologies.

    The individual country histories are often fascinating in their own right, highlighting that virtually no country has escaped unscathed from economic crises of one form or another. In effect, in a number of countries, financial crises are more "a way of life" affecting all, if not most, generations. Black swans are not that rare.

    The prologue to this chartbook is minimalist by design and is organized as follows. The next section offers an essential guide to the country charts and the accompanying tables, clarifies methodological issues, and delineates the approach followed to document the vast number of sources referenced in this analysis.

    Section III summarizes some of the main (common or recurrent) themes and patterns that (collectively) the country histories reveal. Some of these are documented in the literature while others merit considerable further study. These "big picture" themes include the repeated-game nature of sovereign debt crises and the fact that serial default is commonplace among today's emerging markets just as it was among advanced economies in an earlier era needs little commentary, as even a casual perusal of the charts display this historical pattern. The serial nature of banking crises (particularly among the more developed economies prior to World War II) is equally compelling. Nearly all of the 21 advanced economies in the sample record an impressive crisis tally, especially from the 1880s to the 1930s. The episodes where there are surges in private debt before the crisis and public debts after the crisis are not only numerous but also span across advanced and emerging-market economies in nearly all regions.

II. Key to Figures and Methodology Notes

For working definitions of banking, currency, debt, and inflation crises, see the extensive discussion in Reinhart and Rogoff (2009 and 2010). As to the crises highlighted in the country profiles, our focus is on primarily external sovereign default (also its less common counterpart—domestic sovereign default) and banking crises. Many countries have a rich history of recurring (and often chronic) exchange rate crashes and inflation crises, particularly (but not exclusively) in post–World War II Latin America. We only provide limited information on these recurring follies in monetary history.[1] We do include, highlight, and date all hyperinflation episodes, as these have been associated with the complete or near complete liquidation (through de facto default) of domestic-currency debts.

Key to Figures

Besides the events discussed above, in a few charts we highlight "near-default" episodes, which involve some form of international assistance to avoid a default or a restructuring. Their dates are also listed in the first column of the accompanying table. Some examples of subsovereign defaults (by states or provinces) are also flagged. In a few figures, historic currency crashes (such as the collapse of an 80-year old peg) are highlighted as well. More mundane episodes of inflation and currency crises are not shown. However, the full sample incidence (share of years) in an inflation crisis is reported in the table below the figure, so as to provide information on chronic inflation problems.[2] The

---

1. In the tables that accompany each country profile, we do provide, as summary statistic on inflation crises, the share of years with annual inflation above 20 per cent per annum. This inflation performance also gives a reasonable indication of the incidence of currency crashes.

2. For evidence on the correlation and overlap between currency crashes and inflation crises, see Reinhart and Rogoff (2010).

major output collapses shown in the tables that accompany the figures and the numerous IMF programs since 1952 (listed as a memorandum item at the bottom of the table) are not depicted in the figures, to avoid compromising clarity.

Insets of Smaller Tables and Charts in Figures

Insets are used throughout to provide complementary information to that shown in the main figure. For example, for many advanced economies, an inset plots household credit to GDP from the mid-1990s to the present to highlight trends in private debts ahead of the 2007–08 crisis. In other cases, these insets provide information on the maturity composition of the debt (public or private, as the case may be) on the eve of a banking crisis, be it default or hyperinflation. The distribution of public and private debt before and after a crisis also provides documentation of the numerous crisis cases where the government assumed important quantities of private debts.

Descriptive Statistics in Tables for Each Country

Descriptive statistics are mostly self-explanatory, but two particulars merit explanation. The first year of banking crises are listed and those shown in *italics* indicate that the episode in question was not deemed to be a systemic crisis. Near-default episodes are also shown in *italics* and not counted in the tally of default. The last column provides information on the largest annual output declines, usually the top five, but more or less when relevant. Both the year and the percent decline (in parentheses) are given. For full output collapse episodes, the interested reader is referred to Barro and Ursua (2008).

The bottom portion of the table gives memorandum items on IMF programs with the country over the period from 1952 to 2009. The first year of the program is listed as well as the total number of programs. The relevant sources are discussed below.

Debt Ratios

Debt is usually shown as a percent of GDP and in a few cases as a percent of exports. In a handful of cases we have debt data for the earlier part of the 19th century but no GDP or trade measure to scale the debt data by. In those few cases, we show changes in debt (often over three years) to provide an indication of the debt cycle. The nominal GDP data come from numerous scholars as well as official statistical sources. For a number of developing countries we have more data on exports than for GDP (in all cases we have post–World War II nominal GDP data). In these cases the figures show the actual debt/GDP ratio for the period during which GDP data are available (say, post-1920s) and use the debt/exports ratio times the average export to GDP ratio (for the period during which both series overlap) to back-cast the series.

References and Sources

Most figures list the main source as Reinhart and Rogoff (2009), which has extensive data appendices listing sources series by series and country by country over different subperiods. Additional sources listed below each figure usually indicate that we came across these sources subsequent to the publication of Reinhart and Rogoff (2009). Prominent examples of the recent discoveries include detailed recent historical studies of Italian, Greek, Dutch, and Swedish public debts (Maura Francese and Angelo Pace for Italy, Sophia Lazaretou on Greek 19th century domestic debts, Frit Bos for the Netherlands, and Klas Fregert and Roger Gustafsson for Sweden.) As the sample was extended to include Bulgaria, Ghana, Iceland, Ireland, and Switzerland, pertinent sources for these are also listed in the relevant country page. Finally, the sources for the IMF programs are Bird, Hussain, and Joyce (2004), Mody and Saravia (2008), and the IMF's Annual Reports for several years to update these studies through 2009.

III. Debt and Crises: Main Themes

This section highlights some of the issues where the collective evidence from the country histories is particularly illuminating. Throughout, we use country examples or specific crises episodes to illustrate particular points.

1. *Serial default is a widespread phenomenon across emerging markets and several advanced economies.* Figures 2.8a and 2.26 for Brazil and Greece, respectively (among many more that are similar), call attention to this point by simply shading the years in default throughout the sample; the summary table also lists the timing and duration of each default spell while the tally entry (bottom of column 1) reports the default tally for 1800–2009. Countries such as France and Spain have a higher count if pre-1800 default episodes are counted.

2. *Prior to World War II, serial banking crises was the norm in the advanced economies but as the larger emerging markets developed a financial sector in the late 1800s, they joined the "serial banking" crisis club.* Country histories for Belgium (figure 2.6), Canada (figure 2.10a), among others, illustrate this pattern. The world financial centers (the United Kingdom, figure 2.65a, and the United States, figure 2.66a) take the lead in serial banking crises. One can speculate that the less-developed economies substitute foreign bankers for nonexistent domestic ones. As such, when acute sovereign fiscal difficulties arise, they become manifest in serial external default rather than serial domestic banking crises.

3. In light of serial debt and banking crises (not to mention chronic currency and price instability), it is not surprising to see a similar *serial pattern in the incidence of IMF programs.* Peru and the Philippines set the record with 24 and 23 programs, respectively. However, IMF programs were not always

in the exclusive domain of emerging markets. During the 1950s–1970s, the IMF was more like the discount window of a central bank and did not carry the stigma of the default or near default cases. Among the advanced economies, IMF programs were far more common during 1950s–early 1980s; the United Kingdom holds the record with 11 programs, and Portugal was the most recent case, with a program in the mid 1980s.[3]

4. *Private debts typically surge prior to banking crises.* This pattern is evident in total external debt (a stock), capital inflow bonanzas (a flow), domestic banking sector credit (a stock), or any combination of these.[4] *Public debts may or may not surge ahead of banking crises.* Indeed, especially in financial repression cases, the government makes efforts to stuff its debts in "captive" bank balance sheets; also, procyclical fiscal policies, where the government amplifies the boom-bust cycle in total debt (as documented in Kaminsky, Reinhart, and Vegh 2005), all too often reinforce the boom in private indebtedness ahead of the banking crisis.

   For external debts, see figures 2.30b and 2.62a for Iceland and Thailand, respectively. Surges in capital inflows do not last forever. When they end, countries often display Calvo-type sudden stop syndrome, even in crises of an earlier century in advanced economies.[5] The US experience during 1865–1913, shown in figure 2.66b, exemplifies this behavior. Domestic credit climbs sharply prior to the banking crisis and unwinds afterward— the examples from banking in Colombia (figure 2.14b) and Norway (figure 2.47b) demonstrate this time profile. By contrast, the famous (or infamous) lost decade and bank debt overhang in post-1992 crisis Japan is evident from figure 2.35b. The coverage on domestic credit boom in this chartbook is not intended to be as comprehensive as public and external debt, which is the primary focus. However, the pattern alluded to here is strongly supported by the evidence from studies that have focused primarily on the domestic credit cycle. The most comprehensive in terms of country coverage is Mendoza and Terrones (2008), who find most booms are followed by currency crises, banking crises, or both. The smaller country set for the 1880–2008 period studied in Schularick and Taylor (2009) presents similar findings.[6]

5. *Banking crises most often either precede or coincide with sovereign debt crises.* To be clear, we are referring to "domestic" banking crises; the issue of whether banking crises in the financial centers precede domestic banking crises and or sovereign defaults or restructurings is examined in some detail in

---

3. Bird et al. (2004) aptly title their paper on IMF programs "Many Happy Returns?"

4. The term "capital flow bonanza" is introduced in Reinhart and Reinhart (2009) and refers to a surge in capital inflows (over and beyond their historic norm).

5. Calvo, Izquierdo, and Loo-Kung (2006), for example.

6. Kaminsky and Reinhart (1999) and Gourinchas, Valdes, and Landerretch (2001) also document for different samples this boom-crisis-bust pattern.

Reinhart and Rogoff (2010). The reasons for this temporal sequence may be the contingent liability story emphasized by Diaz-Alejandro (1985) and formalized in Velasco (1987), in which the government takes on massive debts from the private banks, thus undermining its solvency.[7] Even absent large-scale bailouts (and without counting the postcrisis new government guarantees), in Reinhart and Rogoff (2009) we establish that largely owing to collapsing revenues, government debts typically rise by about 86 percent in the three years following a systemic financial crisis. This sets the stage for rating downgrades and, in the worst scenario, default.

The list of country examples of this sequencing is too long to enumerate, and we would highlight as illustrative the Barings 1891 crisis in Argentina (figure 2.3b), Austria's banking crisis in 1931 and subsequent default in 1932 (figure 2.5a), and Indonesia's 1997–98 banking crisis and 1999–2000 default (figure 2.32a).

6. *Public debts follow a repeated boom-bust cycle; many (if not most) of the bust phase involved a debt crisis in emerging markets. Public-sector borrowing surges as the crisis nears.* Debts continue to rise after default, as arrears accumulate and GDP contracts markedly.[8] If there is an exchange rate crash associated with default, as shown in Reinhart (2002), the valuation effect on external debts also contributes to further increase in debt/GDP ratios.

The boom-bust episodes are very numerous cutting across regions and time. The crisis episode in figure 2.69 for Zambia illustrates the precrisis surge in public debt—as well as its continued climb in the early stage of default.

7. As Douglas Diamond and Philip Dybvig (1983) suggest in their famous framework of banking crises, *short-term debts (public and private) escalate on the eve of banking crisis and sovereign defaults.*[9] This pattern is also consistent with He and Xiong's (2010) setting, where creditors have incentives to shorten debt maturity to protect themselves against runs by other creditors. Most famously, Mexico ramped up its short-term debt issuance just in advance of its "Tesobonos" crisis in 1994, as shown in figure 2.40b. In the march toward hyperinflation, long-term debts disappear altogether; the German hyperinflation of 1923–24 (figure 2.24a) demonstrates these dynamics.

8. *Private debts become public debts—after the crisis.* Several examples from the debt crisis that engulfed Latin America in the early 1980s and lasted a decade are documented in various insets that document the rising share of private "hidden debts" carrying implicit government guarantees (figure 2.62a for Thailand, among others; figure 2.19b for Ecuador, for example).[10]

---

7. See Arellano and Kocherlakota (2008) for a framework that is consistent with these dynamics.

8. See Reinhart and Rogoff (2008) for evidence on output behavior before, during, and after debt crises.

9. See Chang and Velasco (2001) for an open-economy treatment of Diamond and Dybvig (1983).

10. For a discussion of hidden public debt see Reinhart and Rogoff (2008).

References

Arellano, Cristina, and Narayana Kocherlakota. 2008. *Internal Debt Crises and Sovereign Defaults.* NBER Working Paper W13794. Cambridge, MA: National Bureau of Economic Research.

Barro, Robert J., and José Ursúa. 2008. *Macroeconomic Crises Since 1870.* NBER Working Paper 13940 (April). Cambridge, MA: National Bureau of Economic Research.

Bassino, Jean-Pascal, and Pierre van del Eng. 2006. New Benchmark of Wages and GDP, 1913–70. Mimeograph. Montpellier University, France.

Bird, G.. M. Hussain, and J. P. Joyce. 2004. Many Happy Returns: Recidivism and the IMF." *Journal of International Money and Finance* 23, no. 2 (March): 231–51.

Bos, F. 2007. *The Dutch Fiscal Framework: History, Current Practice and the Role of the CPB.* CPB Document 150. The Hague: CPB Netherlands Bureau for Economic Policy Analysis.

Butlin, S. J. 1968. *Foundations of the Australian Monetary System, 1788–1851.* Sydney: Sydney University Press.

Calvo, Guillermo A., Alejandro Izquierdo, and Rudy Loo-Kung. 2006. Relative Price Volatility Under Sudden Stops: The Relevance of Balance Sheet Effects. *Journal of International Economics* 9, no. 1: 231–54.

Chang, Roberto, and Andres Velasco. 2001. A Model of Financial Crises in Emerging Markets. *Quarterly Journal of Economics* 116, no. 2: 489–517.

Creutzberg, P. 1976. *Changing Economy in Indonesia, Volume 2: Public Finance 1816–1939.* The Hague: Martinus Nijhoff.

Diamond, Douglas, and Philip Dybvig. 1983. Bank Runs, Deposit Insurance, and Liquidity. *Journal of Political Economy* 91, no. 3 (June): 401–19.

Diaz-Alejandro, Carlos. 1985. Goodbye Financial Repression, Hello Financial Crash. *Journal of Development Economics* 19.

Diaz, José B., Rolf Lüders, and Gert Wagner. 2005. Chile, 1810–2000, La Republica en Cifras. Instituto de Economía, Pontificia Universidad Católica de Chile, Santiago. Mimeo (May).

Eitrheim, Ø., K. Gerdrup, and J. T. Klovland. 2004. Credit, Banking and Monetary Developments in Norway 1819–2003. In *Historical Monetary Statistics for Norway, 1819–2003*, ed. Ø. Eitrheim, J. T. Klovland, and J. F. Qvigstad. Norges Bank Occasional Papers no. 35: 377–408.

Francese Maura, and Angelo Pace. 2008. *Il debito pubblico italiano dall'Unità a oggi. Una ricostruzione della serie storica.* Banca d'Italia Occasional Paper no. 31. Rome.

Fregert, K., and R. Gustafsson. 2008. Fiscal Statistics for Sweden 1719–2003. *Research in Economic History* 25: 137–91.

Gold, Joseph. 1970. *Stand-By Arrangements of the International Monetary Fund.* Washington: International Monetary Fund.

Gourinchas, Pierre-Olivier, Rodrigo Valdes, and Oscar Landerretch. 2001. Lending Booms: Latin America and the World. *Economia* (Spring): 47–99.

Hanke, Steve H. 2008. *New Hyperinflation Index (HHIZ) Puts Zimbabwe Inflation at 89.7 Sextillion Percent.* Washington: Cato Institute (November). Available at www.cato.org/zimbabwe

He, Zhiguo, and Wei Xiong. 2010. Dynamic Debt Runs. Mimeograph. University of Chicago and Princeton University, February.

Government Offices of Iceland. 2010. *Historical Statistics of Iceland.* Available at http://www2.stjr.is/frr/thst/rit/sogulegt/english.htm#8.

Junguito, Roberto, and Hernán Rincón. 2004. *La política fiscal en el siglo XX en Colombia.* Borradores de Economía, no. 318. Banco de la República.

Kaminsky, Graciela L., and Carmen M. Reinhart. 1999. The Twin Crises: The Causes of Banking and Balance of Payments Problems. *American Economic Review* 89, no.4 (June): 473–500.

Kaminsky, Graciela, Carmen M. Reinhart, and Carlos A. Végh. 2005. When It Rains, It Pours: Procyclical Capital Flows and Policies. In *NBER Macroeconomics Annual 2004*, volume 19, ed. Mark Gertler and Kenneth S. Rogoff. Cambridge, MA: MIT Press.

Kostelenos, G., S. Petmezas et al. 2007. Gross Domestic Product 1830–1939. *Sources of Economic History of Modern Greece*. Historical Archives of the National Bank of Greece.

Lazaretou, Sophia. 2005. Greek Monetary Economics in Retrospect: The Adventures of the Drachma. *Economic Notes by Banca Monte dei Paschi di Siena* 34, no. 3: 331–70.

Levandis, John Alexander. 1944. *The Greek Foreign Debt and the Great Powers, 1821–1898*. New York: Columbia University Press.

Mendoza, Enrique G., and Marco E. Terrones. 2008. *An Anatomy of Credit Booms: Evidence from macro Aggregates and Micro Data*. NBER Working Paper 14049 (May). Cambridge, MA: National Bureau of Economic Research.

Mody, Ashoka, and Diego Saravia. 2008. *From Crisis to IMF-Supported Program: Does Democracy Impede the Speed Required by Financial Markets?* IMF Working Paper 08/276. Washington: International Monetary Fund.

National Treasury Management Agency (Ireland). 2010. *National Debt of Ireland: 1923–2009*. Available at http://www.ntma.ie/NationalDebt/historicalData1.php.

Pamuk, Sevket. 1995. *Ottoman Foreign Trade in the 19th Century*. Historical Statistics Series, Volume 1. Ankara: State Institute of Statistics.

Reinhart, Carmen M. 2002. Default, Currency Crises, and Sovereign Credit Ratings. *World Bank Economic Review* 16, no. 2: 151–70.

Reinhart, Carmen M., and Vincent R. Reinhart. 2009. Capital Flow Bonanzas: An Encompassing View of the Past and Present. In *NBER International Seminar in Macroeconomics 2008*, ed. Jeffrey Frankel and Francesco Giavazzi. Chicago: Chicago University Press for NBER.

Reinhart, Carmen M., and Rogoff, Kenneth S. 2008. *The Forgotten History of Domestic Debt*. NBER Working Paper 13946 (April). Cambridge, MA: National Bureau of Economic Research.

Reinhart, Carmen M., and Kenneth S. Rogoff. 2009. *This Time is Different: Eight Centuries of Financial Folly*. Princeton: Princeton Press.

Reinhart, Carmen M., and Kenneth S. Rogoff. 2010. *From Financial Crash to Debt Crisis*. NBER Working Paper 15795. Cambridge, MA: National Bureau of Economic Research.

Schularick, Moritz, and Alan M. Taylor. 2009. *Credit Booms Gone Bust: Monetary Policy, Leverage Cycles, and Financial Crises, 1870–2008*. NBER Working Paper 15512. Cambridge, MA: National Bureau of Economic Research.

Soley Güell, Tomas. 1926. *Historia Monetaria de Costa Rica*. San Jose, Costa Rica: Imprenta Nacional.

Stone, Irving. 1999. *The Global Export of Capital from Great Britain, 1865–1914*. New York: St. Martin's Press.

UKpublicspending. 2010. *Public Spending in the United Kingdom*. Available at www.ukpublicspending.co.uk.

Velasco, Andres. 1987. Financial and Balance-of-Payments Crises. *Journal of Development Economics* 27, no. 1/2 (October: 263–83.

Yousef, Tarik M. 2002. Egypt's Growth Performance Under Economic Liberalism: A Reassessment with New GDP Estimates, 1886–1945. *Review of Income and Wealth* 48 (December): 561–79.

Figure 2.1 Algeria: External (public plus private) debt, default, and banking crises, 1970–2009

debt as a percent of GDP

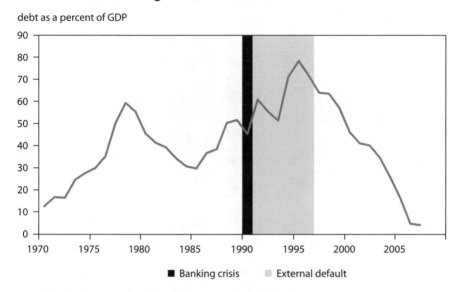

■ Banking crisis   ▨ External default

Sources: Reinhart and Rogoff (2009) and sources cited therein.

Table 2.1 Algeria: Default, restructuring, banking crises, growth collapses, and IMF programs, 1962–2009

External default/ restructuring	Duration (in years)	Domestic default/ restructuring	Banking crisis dates (first year)	Hyper- inflation dates	Share of years in external default	Share of years in inflation crisis	5 worst output collapses, year (decline)
1991–96	6	n.a.	1990	n.a.	10.4	12.5	1961 (12.1)
							1962 (21.1)
							1966 (4.8)
Number of episodes:							1971 (8.5)
1		0	1	0			1980 (5.4)

Memorandum item on IMF programs, 1952–2009	
Dates of programs	Total number
1989, 1991, 1994, 1995	4

n.a. = not applicable

Figure 2.2　Angola: External (public plus private) debt, default, hyperinflation, and banking crises, 1975–2009

debt as a percent of GDP

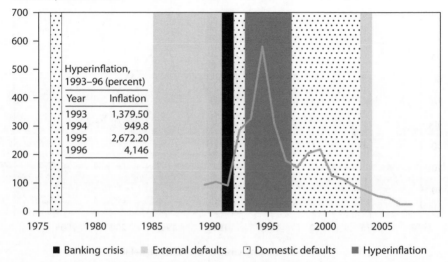

Hyperinflation,
1993–96 (percent)

Year	Inflation
1993	1,379.50
1994	949.8
1995	2,672.20
1996	4,146

■ Banking crisis　　■ External defaults　　☐ Domestic defaults　　■ Hyperinflation

Notes: No data are available prior to 1985 right after independence from Portugal (1975) and during the early years of the 27-year civil war (1975–2002).

Sources: Reinhart and Rogoff (2009) and sources cited therein.

Table 2.2　Angola: Default, restructuring, banking crises, growth collapses, hyperinflation, and IMF programs, 1975–2009

External default/ restructuring	Duration (in years)	Domestic default/ restructuring	Banking crisis dates (first year)	Hyper-inflation dates	Share of years in external default	Share of years in inflation crisis	5 worst output collapses, year (decline)
1985–2003	19	1976	*1991*	1993–96	54.3	60	1974 (5.0)
		1992–2002					1975 (38.4)
							1976 (10.2)
Number of episodes:							1992 (5.8)
1		2	1	1			1993 (24.0)

Memorandum item on IMF programs, 1952–2009	
Dates of programs	Total
None	0

Note: Banking crisis years shown in *italics* indicate that the episode was not deemed to be a systemic crisis.

Figure 2.3a   Argentina: Central government (domestic plus external) debt, default, hyperinflation, and banking crises, 1824–2009

debt as a percent of GDP

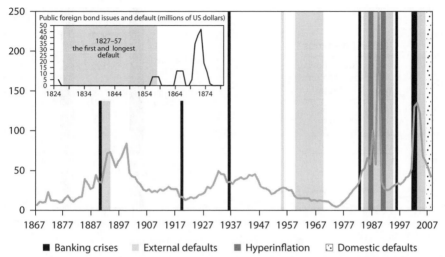

■ Banking crises   ▨ External defaults   ■ Hyperinflation   ⊡ Domestic defaults

Notes: Only systemic banking crises are shown above. Domestic default episodes that overlap with external default are not shaded (see table 2.3 below for dates).

Sources: Reinhart and Rogoff (2009) and sources cited therein.

Table 2.3   Argentina: Default, restructuring, banking crises, growth collapses, hyperinflation, and IMF programs, 1816–2009

External default/ restructuring	Duration (in years)	Domestic default/ restructuring	Banking crisis dates (first year)	Hyper-inflation dates	Share of years in external default	Share of years in inflation crisis	7 worst output collapses, year (decline)
1827–57	31	1890–93	*1885*	1984–85	32.5	24.7	1914 (10.4)
1890–93	4	1982	1890	1989–90			1917 (8.1)
1951	1	1989–90	1914				1931 (6.9)
1956–65	10	2001–05	1931				1959 (6.5)
1982–93	12	2007–09	1934				1985 (7.0)
1989	—		1980				1989 (7.0)
2001–05	9		*1985*				2002 (10.9)
			1989				
			1995				
			2001				
Number of episodes:							
7		5	10	2			

Memorandum item on IMF programs, 1952–2009
Dates of programs   Total
1958–62, 1967–68, 1976–77, 1983–84, 1987, 1989, 1991–92, 1996, 1998, 2000, 2003(2)   20

Note: Banking crisis years shown in *italics* indicate that the episode was not deemed to be a systemic crisis.

Figure 2.3b Argentina: Private capital inflows from the United Kingdom, default, devaluation, and banking crises, 1865–95

capital flows as a percent of exports

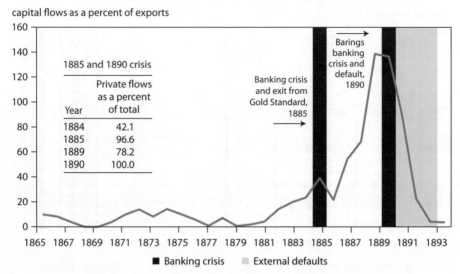

Banking crisis ■ *External defaults* ▨

Sources: Stone (1999), Reinhart and Rogoff (2009) and sources cited therein.

Figure 2.3c Argentina banking survey: Domestic credit, default, hyperinflation, and banking crises, 1970–2008

credit outstanding at end of period as a percent of GDP, 4-quarter moving average

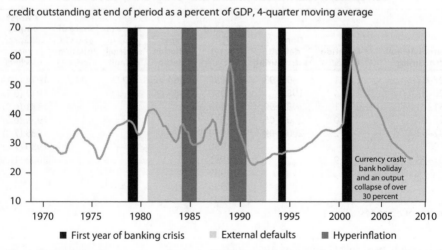

■ *First year of banking crisis* ▨ *External defaults* ■ *Hyperinflation*

Notes: For periods where no quarterly nominal GDP is available, a moving-average interpolation method is used. Only systemic banking crises are shown.

Sources: International Monetary Fund, *International Financial Statistics;* Reinhart and Rogoff (2009); and sources cited therein.

Figure 2.4a   Australia: Central government (domestic plus external) debt, near-default, and banking crises, 1852–2009

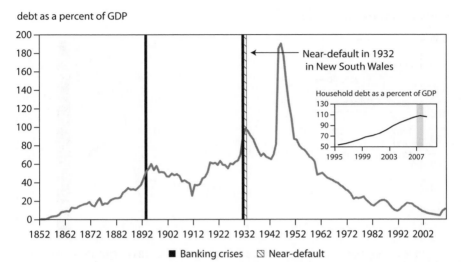

Notes: An interesting anecdote on sub-sovereign debt from correspondence with Huw McKay (who also referred us to Butlin's work, which dates the earliest banking crises): During the Great Depression, the left-wing government of the largest state in Australia, New South Wales, voted to default on its foreign debt, only to be overruled by the federal government. Only systemic banking crises are shown.

Sources: Butlin (1968); OECD; Reinhart and Rogoff (2009) and sources cited therein.

Table 2.4   Australia: Default, restructuring, banking crises, growth collapses, and IMF programs, 1800–2010 (calculations since independence—1901)

External default/ restructuring	Duration (in years)	Domestic default/ restructuring	Banking crisis dates (first year)	Hyper-inflation dates	Share of years in external default	Share of years in inflation crisis	5 worst output collapses, year (decline)
1932	n.a.	1932	1828	n.a.	n.a.	2.8	1882 (5.6)
			1843				1892 (12.3)
			1893				1893 (5.5)
			1931				1930 (9.5)
			1989				1931 (6.7)
Number of episodes:							
0		1	5	0			

Memorandum item on IMF programs, 1952–2009
Dates of programs   Total
1961   1

n.a. = not applicable

Notes: Near external default *(italics)* not counted in total; domestic debt "forcible" conversion. Banking crisis years shown in *italics* indicate that the episode was not deemed to be a systemic crisis. See also notes in figure 2.4a.

Figure 2.4b   Australia: Private capital inflows from the United Kingdom and banking crises, 1865–95

capital flows as a percent of exports

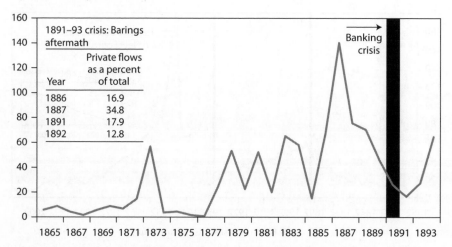

Sources: Stone (1999), Reinhart and Rogoff (2009) and sources cited therein.

Figure 2.5a   Austria: Central government (domestic plus external) debt, default, and banking crises, 1880–2009

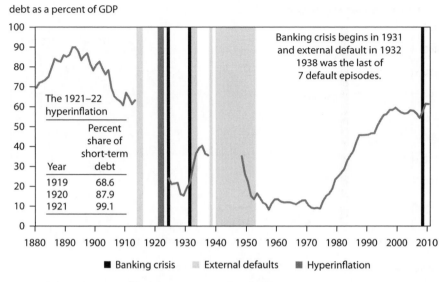

debt as a percent of GDP

The 1921–22 hyperinflation

Year	Percent share of short-term debt
1919	68.6
1920	87.9
1921	99.1

Banking crisis begins in 1931 and external default in 1932 1938 was the last of 7 default episodes.

■ Banking crisis   ▨ External defaults   ■ Hyperinflation

Sources: Reinhart and Rogoff (2009) and sources cited therein.

Table 2.5   Austria: Default, restructuring, banking crises, growth collapses, hyperinflation, and IMF programs, 1800–2009
(Austria-Hungary pre-1918)

External default/ restructuring	Duration (in years)	Domestic default/ restructuring	Banking crisis dates (first year)	Hyper-inflation dates	Share of years in external default	Share of years in inflation crisis	4 worst output collapses, year (decline)[1]
1802–15	14	1945	1873	1921–22	17.1	13.3	1919 (15.6)
1816	1		1924				1931 (8.0)
1868–70	3		1929				1932 (10.3)
1914–15	2		1931				*2009 (3.8)*
1932–33	2		2008				
1938	1						
1940–52	13						
Number of episodes:							
7		1	5	1			

Memorandum item on IMF programs, 1952–2009
Dates of programs   Total
None   0

1. Excludes World Wars I and II.

Notes: There is an issue whether to treat (more or less) consecutive defaults in 1802, 1805, and 1811 as separate episodes or as a single longer episode, as above. Summary of private forecasts for 2009 in *italics*.

Figure 2.5b   Austria: Private capital inflows from the United Kingdom and banking crises, 1865–1914

capital flows as a percent of exports

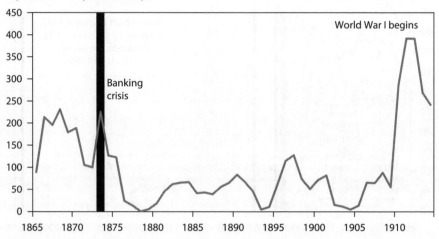

Sources: Stone (1999), Reinhart and Rogoff (2009) and sources cited therein.

Figure 2.6 Belgium: Central government (domestic plus external) debt and banking crises, 1835–2009

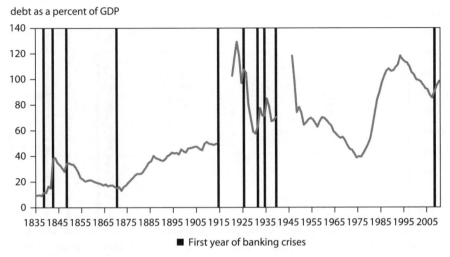

debt as a percent of GDP

■ First year of banking crises

Sources: Reinhart and Rogoff (2009) and sources cited therein.

Table 2.6 Belgium: Default, restructuring, banking crises, growth collapses, and IMF programs, 1800–2009

External default/ restructuring	Duration (in years)	Domestic default/ restructuring	Banking crisis dates (first year)	Hyper- inflation dates	Share of years in external default	Share of years in inflation crisis	3 worst output collapses, year (decline)[1]
n.a.	n.a.	n.a.	1838	n.a.	n.a.	5.2	1932 (4.5)
			1842				1938 (2.3)
			1848				*2009 (3.2)*
			1870				
			1914				
			1925				
			1931				
			1934				
			1939				
			2008				
Number of episodes:							
0		0	10	0			

Memorandum item on IMF programs, 1952–2009
Dates of programs   Total
1952   1

n.a. = not applicable

1. Excludes World Wars I and II.

Notes: Summary of private forecasts for 2009 in *italics*.

Figure 2.7 Bolivia: Central government (domestic plus external) debt, default, banking crises, and hyperinflation, 1914–2009

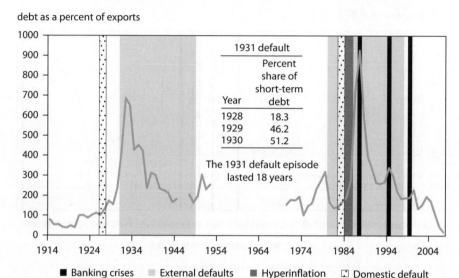

debt as a percent of exports

1931 default

Year	Percent share of short-term debt
1928	18.3
1929	46.2
1930	51.2

The 1931 default episode lasted 18 years

■ Banking crises   ▨ External defaults   ■ Hyperinflation   ☐ Domestic default

Notes: No GDP data are available prior to 1950, hence we scale debt by exports.

Sources: Reinhart and Rogoff (2009) and sources cited therein; UNCTAD Handbook of Statistics.

Table 2.7 Bolivia: Default, restructuring, banking crises, growth collapses, hyperinflation, and IMF programs, 1825–2009

External default/ restructuring	Duration (in years)	Domestic default/ restructuring	Banking crisis dates (first year)	Hyper- inflation dates	Share of years in external default	Share of years in inflation crisis	4 worst output collapses, year (decline)
1875–79	5	1927	1987	1984–85	21.6	14.6	1954 (9.5)
1931–48	18	1982–85	1994				1956 (5.9)
1980–84	5		*1999*				1982 (4.4)
1986–93	8						1983 (4.5)
1989–97	9						
Number of episodes:							
5		2	3	1			

Memorandum item on IMF programs, 1952–2009
Dates of programs   Total
1956–57, 1959, 1961–67, 1969, 1973, 1980, 1986 (2), 1988(2), 1994, 1998, 2001   20

Figure 2.8a Brazil: External debt, default, hyperinflation, and banking crises, 1824–2009

debt as a percent of exports

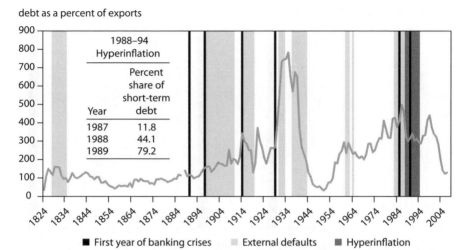

■ First year of banking crises   ▒ External defaults   ■ Hyperinflation

Notes: For 1824–1945, public external debt; for 1946–2009 external debt is the aggregate of public and private debts. There are a total of 9 default episodes but only 8 shaded regions, as two episodes occur in consecutive years (see table 2.8). Only the major, systemic banking crises are shown.

Sources: Reinhart and Rogoff (2009) and sources cited therein.

Table 2.8 Brazil: Default, restructuring, banking crises, growth collapses, hyperinflation, and IMF programs, 1822–2009

External default/ restructuring	Duration (in years)	Domestic default/ restructuring	Banking crisis dates (first year)	Hyper-inflation dates	Share of years in external default	Share of years in inflation crisis	5 worst output collapses, year (decline)
1828–34	7	1986–87	1890	1988–90	26.6	26.1	1893 (12.8)
1898–01	4	1990	1897	1992–94			1896 (7.2)
1902–10	9		1900	*or*			1930 (6.0)
1914–19	6		1914	*single*			1981 (4.4)
1931–33	3		1923	*episode*			1990 (4.2)
1937–43	7		1926	1988–94			
1961	1		1929				
1964	1		*1963*				
1983–90	8		1985				
			1990				
			1994				
Number of episodes:							
9		2	11	2(1)			

Memorandum item on IMF programs, 1952–2009
Dates of programs   Total
1958, 1961, 1965–72, 1983, 1988, 1992, 1998, 2001–02   16

Figure 2.8b Brazil: Private capital inflows from the United Kingdom and default and banking crises, 1875–1914

capital flows as a percent of exports

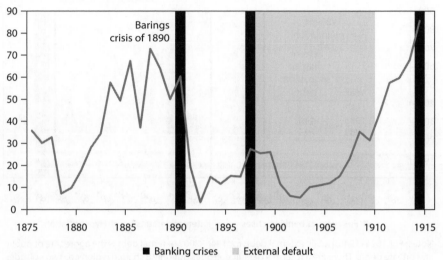

Sources: Stone (1999), Reinhart and Rogoff (2009) and sources cited therein.

Figure 2.9 Bulgaria: Central government (domestic plus external) debt, default, and banking crises, 1919–2009

debt as a percent of GDP

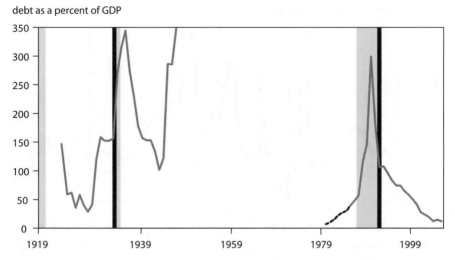

■ Banking crises ▦ Three external defaults ▬▬▬1981–90, only external public debt data available

Sources: Reinhart and Rogoff (2009) and sources cited therein.

Table 2.9 Bulgaria: Default, restructuring, banking crises, growth collapses, and IMF programs, 1916–2009

External default/ restructuring	Duration (in years)	Domestic default/ restructuring	Banking crisis dates (first year)	Hyper-inflation dates	Share of years in external default	Share of years in inflation crisis	6 worst output collapses, year (decline)
1916–20	5	n.a.	1931	n.a.	n.a.		1934 (8.5)
1932	1		1994				1990 (9.1)
1990–94	5						1991 (10.8)
							1993 (11.6)
Number of episodes:							1996 (8.0)
3		0	2	0			*2009 (6.5)*

Memorandum item on IMF programs, 1952–2009
Dates of programs
1991–92, 1994, 1996–98, 2002, 2004

Total number
8

n.a. = not applicable

Notes: Summary of private forecasts for 2009 in *italics*.

Figure 2.10a   Canada: Central government (domestic plus external), 1867–2009

debt as a percent of exports and GDP

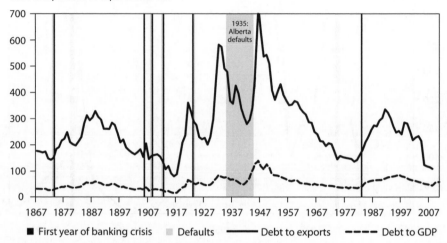

■ First year of banking crisis   ▨ Defaults   —— Debt to exports   ---- Debt to GDP

Note: The 1983 banking crisis (also shown) does not meet the systemic criteria.

Sources: Reinhart and Rogoff (2009) and sources cited therein.

Table 2.10   Canada: Default, restructuring, banking crises, growth collapses, and IMF programs, 1867–2009

External default/ restructuring	Duration (in years)	Domestic default/ restructuring	Banking crisis dates (first year)	Hyper-inflation dates	Share of years in external default	Share of years in inflation crisis	6 worst output collapses, year (decline)
1935 "near"	10	n.a.	1837	n.a.	n.a.	0.7	1876 (6.7)
			1866				1919 (7.6)
			1873				1921 (10.8)
			1906				1931 (15.4)
			1908				1932 and
							1933 (7.1)
			1912				
			1923				
			1983				
Number of episodes:							
0		0	8	0			

Memorandum item on IMF programs, 1952–2009
Dates of programs   Total
None   0

n.a. = not applicable

Note: Banking crisis years shown in *italics* indicate that the episode was not deemed to be a systemic crisis.

**Figure 2.10b Canada: Private capital inflows from the United Kingdom
and banking crises, 1865–1914**

capital flows as a percent of exports

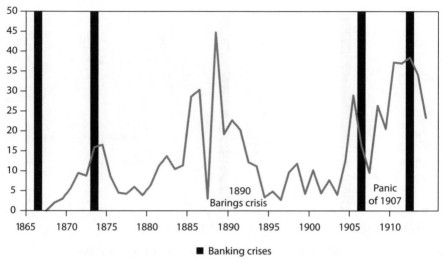

1890
Barings crisis

Panic
of 1907

■ Banking crises

Sources: Stone (1999), Reinhart and Rogoff (2009) and sources cited therein.

Figure 2.11   Central African Republic: External (public plus private) debt, default, devaluation, and banking crises, 1970–2009

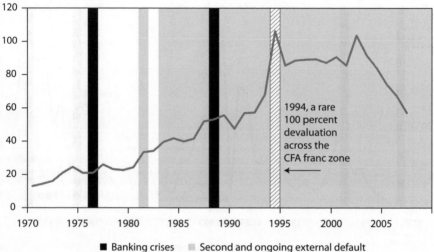

debt as a percent of GDP

1994, a rare 100 percent devaluation across the CFA franc zone ←

■ Banking crises   ▨ Second and ongoing external default

Sources: Reinhart and Rogoff (2009) and sources cited therein.

Table 2.11   Central African Republic: Default, restructuring, banking crises, growth collapses, and IMF programs, 1960–2009

External default/ restructuring	Duration (in years)	Domestic default/ restructuring	Banking crisis dates (first year)	Hyper-inflation dates	Share of years in external default	Share of years in inflation crisis	4 worst output collapses, year (decline)
1981	1	n.a.	1976	n.a.	56	4	1979 (5.6)
1983–09	27		1988				1983 (6.0)
Number of episodes:							1996 (8.1)
2		0	2	0			2003 (7.1)

Memorandum item on IMF programs, 1952–09	
Dates of programs	Total
1980–81, 1983–85, 1987(2), 1989, 1994, 1998	10

n.a. = not applicable

Figure 2.12a   Chile: Central government (domestic plus external) debt, default, and banking crises, 1826–2009

debt as a percent of GDP

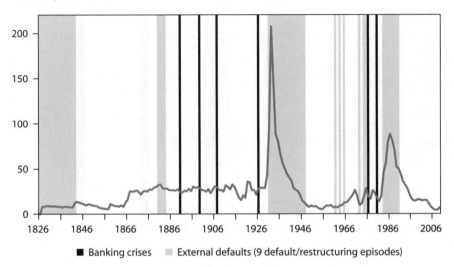

■ Banking crises   ▨ External defaults (9 default/restructuring episodes)

Sources: Diaz, Lüder, and Wagner (2005), Reinhart and Rogoff (2009) and sources cited therein.

Table 2.12   Chile: Default, banking crises, restructuring, growth collapses, and IMF programs, 1818–2009

External default/ restructuring	Duration (in years)	Domestic default/ restructuring	Banking crisis dates (first year)	Hyper- inflation dates	Share of years in external default	Share of years in inflation crisis	8 worst output collapses, year (decline)
1826–42	16	n.a.	1890	n.a.	27.1	20.3	1919 (14.2)
1880–83	4		1899				1921 (13.3)
1931–47	18		1907				1930 (16.0)
1961	1		1915				1931 (21.2)
1963	1		1926				1932 (15.5)
1965	1		1976				1947 (10.8)
1972	1		1981				1975 (12.9)
1974–75	2						1982 (13.6)
1983–90	8						
Number of episodes:							
9		0	7	0			

Memorandum item on IMF programs, 1952–2009
Dates of programs   Total
1956, 1958–59, 1961, 1963–66, 1968–69, 1974–75, 1983, 1985, 1989 (2)   16

n.a. = not applicable

Figure 2.12b   Chile: Total (public and private) capital inflows from the United Kingdom, default, and banking crises, 1865–1914

capital flows as a percent of exports, three-year sum

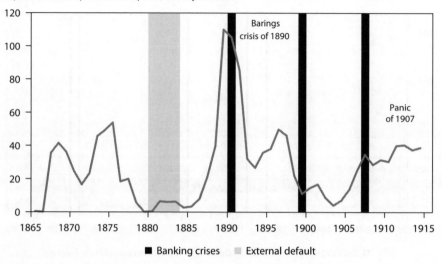

Sources: Stone (1999), Reinhart and Rogoff (2009) and sources cited therein.

Figure 2.13a   China: Central government (domestic plus external) debt, default, and banking crises, 1885–1937

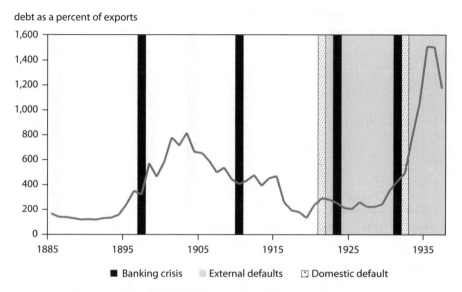

debt as a percent of exports

■ Banking crisis   ▨ External defaults   ⬚ Domestic default

Sources: Reinhart and Rogoff (2009) and sources cited therein.

Table 2.13   China: Default, restructuring, banking crises, growth collapses, hyperinflation, and IMF programs, 1850–2009

External default/ restructuring	Duration (in years)	Domestic default/ restructuring	Banking crisis dates (first year)	Hyper-inflation dates	Share of years in external default	Share of years in inflation crisis	3 worst output collapses, year (decline)[1]
1921–36	16	1921	1863	1946–48	12.9	10	1934 (8.7)
1939–49	11	1932	1866				1960 (3.4)
			1873				1961 (17.3)
			1883				
			1898				
			1910				
			1923				
			1931				
			1934				
Number of episodes:			1998				
2		2	10	1			

Memorandum item on IMF programs, 1952–2009
Dates of programs   Total
1981, 1986   2

1. No output data from 1939 to 1951.

Figure 2.13b China: Public and private capital inflows from the United Kingdom and banking crises, 1875–1914

capital flows as a percent of exports, three-year sum

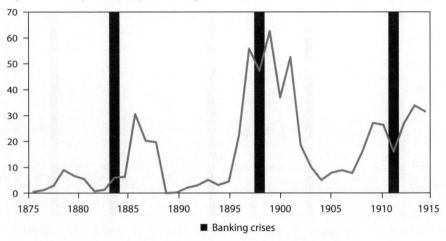

■ Banking crises

Sources: Stone (1999), Reinhart and Rogoff (2009) and sources cited therein.

Figure 2.13c China: Central government debt issuance (domestic plus external) and banking crises, 1981–2009

three-year sum in issuance as a percent of GDP

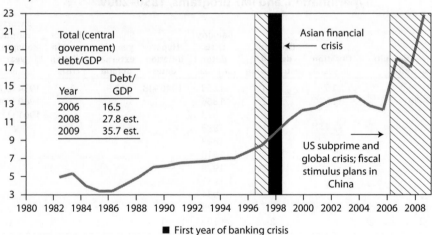

■ First year of banking crisis

Notes: Data on central government debt outstanding (domestic plus external) are no longer published. Estimates for 2008 and 2009 are based on issuance data for those years.

Sources: China Statistical Yearbook, several issues; National Debt Association of China; Reinhart and Rogoff (2009) and sources cited therein; and authors' calculations.

Figure 2.14a   Colombia: Central government (domestic plus external) debt, default, and banking crises, 1902–2009

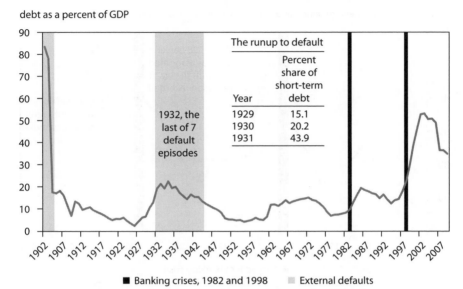

debt as a percent of GDP

The runup to default

Year	Percent share of short-term debt
1929	15.1
1930	20.2
1931	43.9

1932, the last of 7 default episodes

■ Banking crises, 1982 and 1998   ▨ External defaults

Sources: Junguito and Rincón (2004), Reinhart and Rogoff (2009) and sources cited therein.

Table 2.14   Colombia: Default, restructuring, banking crises, growth collapses, and IMF programs, 1819–2009

External default/ restructuring	Duration (in years)	Domestic default/ restructuring	Banking crisis dates (first year)	Hyper-inflation dates	Share of years in external default	Share of years in inflation crisis	3 worst output collapses, year (decline)
1826–45	20	n.a.	1982	n.a.	35.6	17.8	1914 (3.4)
1850–61	12		1998				1934 (2.1)
1873	1						1999 (4.2)
1880–96	17						
1900–04	5						
1932–34	3						
1935–44	10						
Number of episodes:							
7		0	2	0			

Memorandum item on IMF programs, 1952–2009
Dates of programs   Total
1957–60, 1962–64, 1966–73, 1999, 2003, 2005   18

n.a. = not applicable

Figure 2.14b   Colombia banking survey: Domestic credit and banking crises, 1970–2008

credit outstanding at end of period as a percent of GDP, 4-quarter moving average

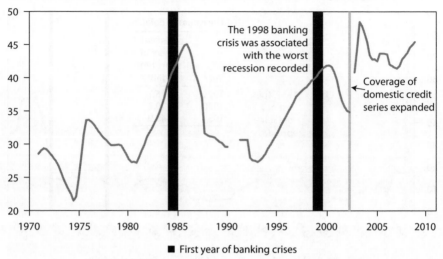

Notes: For periods where no quarterly nominal GDP is available, a moving-average interpolation method is used.

Sources: International Monetary Fund, *International Financial Statistics;* Reinhart and Rogoff (2009) and sources cited therein.

Figure 2.15 Costa Rica: Central government (domestic plus external) debt default and banking crises, 1892–2009

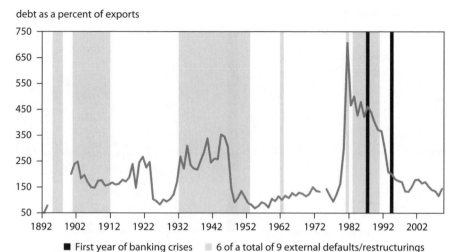

debt as a percent of exports

■ First year of banking crises   ▨ 6 of a total of 9 external defaults/restructurings

Notes: No GDP data are available prior to 1950; hence we scale debt by exports.

Sources: Soley Güell (1926), UNCTAD Handbook of Statistics, Reinhart and Rogoff (2009) and sources cited therein.

Table 2.15 Costa Rica: Default, restructuring, banking crises, growth collapses, and IMF programs, 1838–2009

External default/ restructuring	Duration (in years)	Domestic default/ restructuring	Banking crisis dates (first year)	Hyper-inflation dates	Share of years in external default	Share of years in inflation crisis	7 worst output collapses, year (decline)
1828–40	13	n.a.	1987	n.a.	34.5	5.3	1923 (7.6)
1874–85	12		1994				1927 (9.2)
1895–97	3						1932 (8.0)
1901–11	11						1934 (11.8)
1932–52	21						1942 (10.4)
1962	1						1944 (9.4)
1981	1						1982 (7.3)
1983–90	8						
1984–85							
Number of episodes:							
9		0	2	0			

Memorandum item on IMF programs, 1952–2009
Dates of programs   Total
1961–62, 1965–67, 1976, 1980–82, 1985, 1987, 1989, 1991, 1993, 1995, 2009   16

n.a. = not applicable

Figure 2.16 Cote D'Ivoire: External (public plus private) debt, default, and banking crises, 1970–2009

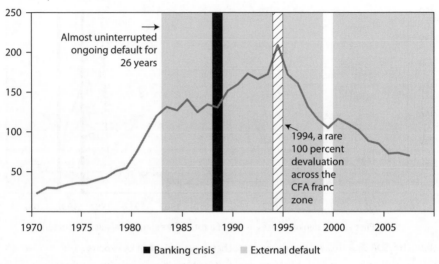

debt as a percent of GDP

Almost uninterrupted ongoing default for 26 years

1994, a rare 100 percent devaluation across the CFA franc zone

■ Banking crisis   ▨ External default

Sources: Reinhart and Rogoff (2009) and sources cited therein.

Table 2.16 Cote D'Ivoire: Default, restructuring, banking crises, growth collapses, and IMF programs, 1960–2009

External default/ restructuring	Duration (in years)	Domestic default/ restructuring	Banking crisis dates (first year)	Hyper- inflation dates	Share of years in external default	Share of years in inflation crisis	4 worst output collapses, year (decline)
1983–98	16	n.a.	1988	n.a.	52	6	1965 (2.2)
2000–09	10						1983 (3.9)
Number of episodes:							1990 (6.9)
2		0	1	0			2000 (4.6)

Memorandum item on IMF programs, 1952–2009
Dates of programs   Total
1981, 1984–86, 1988–89, 1991, 1994, 1998, 2002, 2009   11

n.a. = not applicable

Figure 2.17 Denmark: Central government (domestic plus external) debt, default, and banking crises, 1880–2009

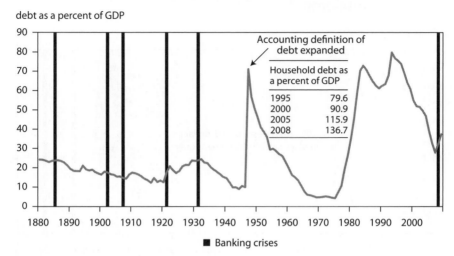

debt as a percent of GDP

Accounting definition of
debt expanded

Household debt as
a percent of GDP

1995	79.6
2000	90.9
2005	115.9
2008	136.7

■ Banking crises

Notes: Only systemic banking crises are shown.

Sources: Reinhart and Rogoff (2009) and sources cited therein.

Table 2.17 Denmark: Default, restructuring, banking crises, growth collapses, and IMF programs, 1800–2009

External default/ restructuring	Duration (in years)	Domestic default/ restructuring	Banking crisis dates (first year)	Hyper-inflation dates	Share of years in external default	Share of years in inflation crisis	5 worst output collapses, year (decline)[1]
n.a.	n.a.	1813	1813	n.a.	0	1.9	1856 (5.6)
			1857				1877 (2.7)
			1877				1921 (2.9)
			1885				1932 (2.6)
			1902				*2009 (5.0)*
			1907				
			1921				
			1931				
			1987				
			2008				
Number of episodes:							
0		1	10	0			

Memorandum item on IMF programs, 1952–2009

Dates of programs   Total number of years

None   0

n.a. = not applicable

1. Excludes World Wars I and II.

Notes: Summary of private forecasts for 2009 in *italics*. Banking crisis years shown in *italics* indicate that the episode was not deemed to be a systemic crisis.

Figure 2.18   Dominican Republic: Central government (domestic plus external) debt, default, devaluation, and banking crises, 1914–2009

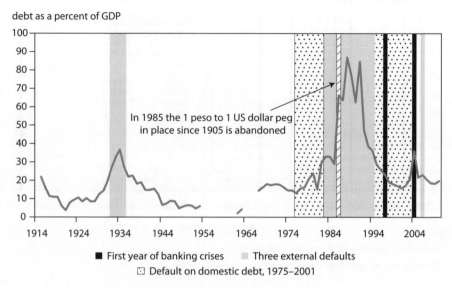

debt as a percent of GDP

In 1985 the 1 peso to 1 US dollar peg in place since 1905 is abandoned

■ First year of banking crises   ▨ Three external defaults
☷ Default on domestic debt, 1975–2001

Sources: Reinhart and Rogoff (2009) and sources cited therein.

Table 2.18   Dominican Republic: Default, restructuring, banking crises, growth collapses, and IMF programs, 1844–2009

External default/ restructuring	Duration (in years)	Domestic default/ restructuring	Banking crisis dates (first year)	Hyper- inflation dates	Share of years in external default	Share of years in inflation crisis	3 worst output collapses, year (decline)
1872–88	17	1975–2001	*1996*	n.a.	28.3	6.6	1965 (12.4)
1892–93	2		2003				1985 (2.5)
1897	1						1990 (5.5)
1899–1907	9						
1931–34	4						
1982–94	13						
2005	1						
Number of episodes:							
7		1	2	0			

Memorandum item on IMF programs, 1952–2009
Dates of programs   Total
1959, 1964, 1983, 1985, 1991, 1993, 2001, 2003, 2005   9

n.a. = not applicable

Note: Banking crisis years shown in *italics* indicate that the episode was not deemed to be a systemic crisis.

Figure 2.19a Ecuador: Central government (domestic plus external) debt, default and banking crises, 1914–2009

debt as a percent of GDP

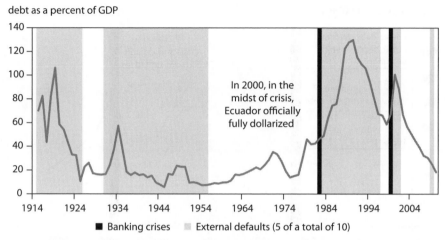

■ Banking crises ▩ External defaults (5 of a total of 10)

Notes: For the period 1973–89 the data are for external public debt for general government. This underestimates public indebtedness, as it does not include domestic (or internal) debts; at the same time general government is more inclusive than our central government measure. These two effects are working in opposite directions.

Sources: Reinhart and Rogoff (2009) and sources cited therein.

Table 2.19 Ecuador: Default, restructuring, banking crises, growth collapses, and IMF programs, 1830–2009

External default/ restructuring	Duration (in years)	Domestic default/ restructuring	Banking crisis dates (first year)	Hyper-inflation dates	Share of years in external default	Share of years in inflation crisis	3 worst output collapses, year (decline)
1826–45	20	1999	1981	n.a.	57.8	13.9	1983 (2.1)
1868–90	4		1998				1987 (6.0)
1894–98	1						1999 (6.3)
1900–04	5						
1906–11	3						
1914–24	9						
1929–54							
1982–95							
1999–2000							
2008							
Number of episodes:							
10		1	2	0			

Memorandum item on IMF programs, 1952–2007
Dates of programs
1961–66, 1969–70, 1983, 1985–86, 1988–89, 1991, 1994, 2000, 2003

Total
18

n.a. = not applicable

Figure 2.19b Ecuador: External (public plus private) debt, default, and banking crises, 1970–2009

debt as a percent of GDP

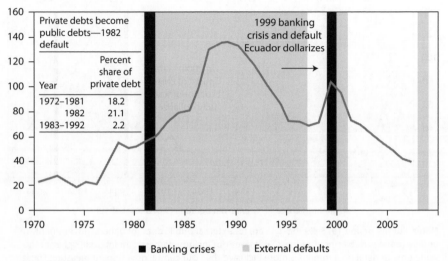

Sources: Reinhart and Rogoff (2009) and sources cited therein.

Figure 2.20   Egypt: Public debt, default, and banking crises, 1862–2009

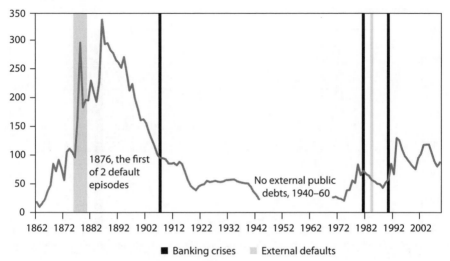

debt as a percent of GDP

1876, the first of 2 default episodes

No external public debts, 1940–60

■ Banking crises   ░ External defaults

Notes: By 1945, the outstanding balance on Ottoman debts were either fully paid off or forgiven; no external debts are recorded through 1960.

Sources: Reinhart and Rogoff (2009) and sources cited therein.

Table 2.20   Egypt: Default, restructuring, banking crises, growth collapses, and IMF programs, 1800–2009

External default/ restructuring	Duration (in years)	Domestic default/ restructuring	Banking crisis dates (first year)	Hyper- inflation dates	Share of years in external default	Share of years in inflation crisis	5 worst output collapses, year (decline)
1876–80	5	n.a.	1907	n.a.	2.9	5.2	1887 (2.2)
1984	1		1981				1914 (3.0)
							1920 (6.6)
Number of episodes:			*1990*				1942 (3.6)
2		0	3	0			1991 (3.2)

Memorandum item on IMF programs, 1952–2009
Dates of programs   Total
1962, 1964, 1977–78, 1987, 1991, 1993, 1996   8

n.a. = not applicable

Note: Banking crisis years shown in *italics* indicate that the episode was not deemed to be a systemic crisis.

Sources: Pre-World War II GDP from Yousef (2002).

Figure 2.21a   El Salvador: Central government (domestic plus external) debt, default and banking crises, 1914–2009

debt as a percent of GDP

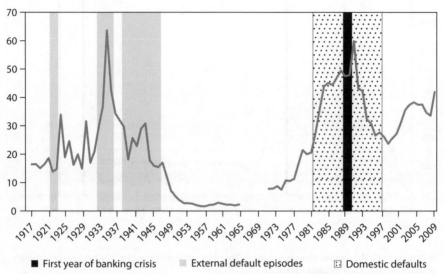

■ First year of banking crisis   ▨ External default episodes   ⊞ Domestic defaults

Notes: No GDP data are available prior to 1950; hence, we scale debt by exports.

Sources: Reinhart and Rogoff (2009), and sources cited therein; UNCTAD Handbook of Statistics.

Table 2.21   El Salvador: Default, restructuring, banking crises, growth collapses, and IMF programs, 1838–2009

External default/ restructuring	Duration (in years)	Domestic default/ restructuring	Banking crisis dates (first year)	Hyper- inflation dates	Share of years in external default	Share of years in inflation crisis	7 worst output collapses, year (decline)
1828–60	33	1981–96	1989	n.a.	22.7	3.5	1927 (12.1)
1898	1						1931 (10.1)
1921–22	3						1932 (10.2)
1932–35	11						1938 (7.1)
1938–46	21						1949 (9.2)
Number of episodes:							1980 (8.6)
5		1	1	0			1982 (6.3)

Memorandum item on IMF programs, 1952–2009
Dates of programs
1958–63, 1965, 1967, 1969–70, 1972, 1980, 1982, 1990, 1992–93, 1995, 1997–98, 2009

Total
20

n.a. = not applicable

Figure 2.21b El Salvador: External (public plus private) debt, default, and banking crises, 1970–2009

debt as a percent of GDP

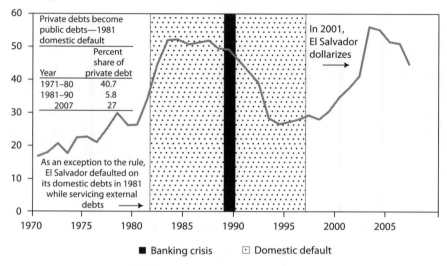

Banking crisis   ⊡ Domestic default

Sources: Reinhart and Rogoff (2009) and sources cited therein.

Figure 2.22a Finland: Central government (domestic plus external) debt and banking crises, 1914–2009

debt as a percent of GDP

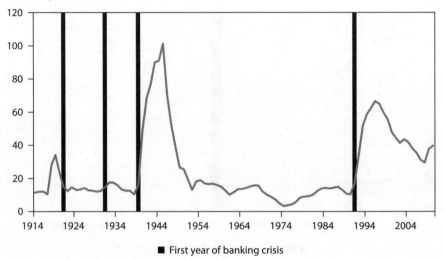

■ First year of banking crisis

Sources: Reinhart and Rogoff (2009) and sources cited therein.

Table 2.22 Finland: Default, restructuring, banking crises, growth collapses, and IMF programs, 1800–2009

External default/ restructuring	Duration (in years)	Domestic default/ restructuring	Banking crisis dates (first year)	Hyper-inflation dates	Share of years in external default	Share of years in inflation crisis	5 worst output collapses, year (decline)[1]
n.a.	n.a.	n.a.	1900	n.a.	n.a.	7.5	1862 (5.4)
			1921				1867 (8.0)
			1931				1931 (2.4)
			1939				1991 (6.2)
			1991				*2009 (6.4)*
Number of episodes:							
0		0	5	0			

Memorandum item on IMF programs, 1952–2009	
Dates of programs	Total
1952, 1967, 1975	3

n.a. = not applicable

1. Excludes World Wars I and II.

Note: Summary of private forecasts for 2009 in *italics*.

Figure 2.22b   Finland banking survey: Domestic credit and banking crises, 1970–2008

credit outstanding at end of period as a percent of GDP, 4-quarter moving average

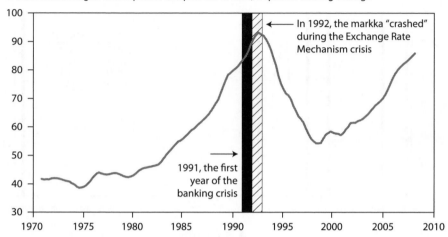

Notes: For periods where no quarterly nominal GDP is available, a moving-average interpolation method is used.

Sources: International Monetary Fund, *International Financial Statistics;* Reinhart and Rogoff (2009) and sources cited therein.

Figure 2.23 France: Central government (domestic plus external) debt and banking crises, 1880–2009

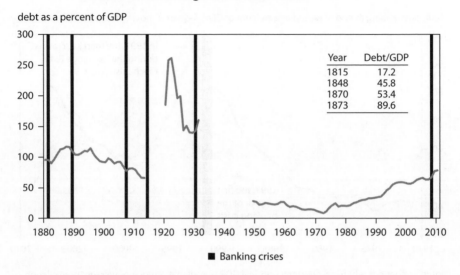

debt as a percent of GDP

Year	Debt/GDP
1815	17.2
1848	45.8
1870	53.4
1873	89.6

■ Banking crises

Sources: Reinhart and Rogoff (2009) and sources cited therein.

Table 2.23 France: Default, restructuring, banking crises, growth collapses, and IMF programs, 1800–2009

External default/ restructuring	Duration (in years)	Domestic default/ restructuring	Banking crisis dates (first year)	Hyper-inflation dates	Share of years in external default	Share of years in inflation crisis	6 worst output collapses, year (decline)[1]
1812	n.a.	n.a.	1802	n.a.	0.5	5.7	1848 (6.1)
			1805				1859 (6.5)
			1848				1870 (7.6)
			1881				1876 (8.2)
			1889				1931 (6.0)
			1907				1932 (6.5)
			1914				
			1930				
			1994				
Number of episodes:							
1		0	9	0			

Memorandum item on IMF programs, 1952–2009
Dates of programs   Total
1956, 1958, 1969   3

n.a. = not applicable

1. Excludes World Wars I and II. There are a couple of additional output declines comparable in magnitude to those shown in the latter 19th century.

Note: Banking crisis years shown in *italics* indicate that the episode was not deemed to be a systemic crisis.

Figure 2.24a Germany: Federal and total government (domestic plus external) debt, default, hyperinflation, and banking crises, 1880–2009

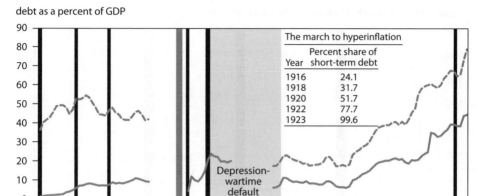

debt as a percent of GDP

The march to hyperinflation

Year	Percent share of short-term debt
1916	24.1
1918	31.7
1920	51.7
1922	77.7
1923	99.6

Depression-wartime default

■ Banking crises   External default   ■ Hyperinflation, 1923–24

- - - - Total public debt ———— Federal debt

Notes: Only systemic banking crises are shown.

Sources: Reinhart and Rogoff (2009) and sources cited therein.

Table 2.24 Germany: Default, restructuring, banking crises, growth collapses, hyperinflation, and IMF programs, 1800–2009

External default/ restructuring	Duration (in years)	Domestic default/ restructuring	Banking crisis dates (first year)	Hyper-inflation dates	Share of years in external default	Share of years in inflation crisis	6 worst output collapses, year (decline)[1]
1807	1	1948	1857	1923–24	12.9	9.5	1919 (19.5)
1812	1		1880				1923 (16.9)
1850	1		1891				1931 (7.6)
1932–53	22		1901				1932 (7.5)
			1925				1946 (52.6)
			1931				*2009 (4.9)*
			1977				
			2007				
Number of episodes:							
4		1	8	1			

Memorandum item on IMF programs, 1952–2009
Dates of programs   Total
None   0

1. Excludes World Wars I and II.

Notes: Summary of private forecasts for 2009 in *italics*. Banking crisis years shown in *italics* indicate that the episode was not deemed to be a systemic crisis.

Figure 2.24b Germany: Public and private capital inflows from the United Kingdom and banking crises, 1870–1912

capital flows as a percent of exports, three-year sum

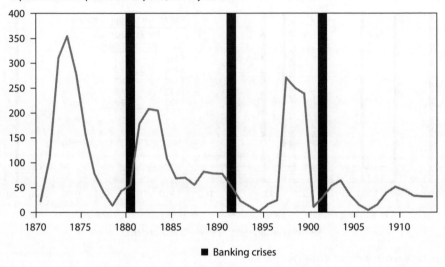

■ Banking crises

Sources: Stone (1999), Reinhart and Rogoff (2009) and sources cited therein.

Figure 2.25 Ghana: Total public (domestic and external) debt, default, and banking crises, 1970–2009

debt as a percent of GDP

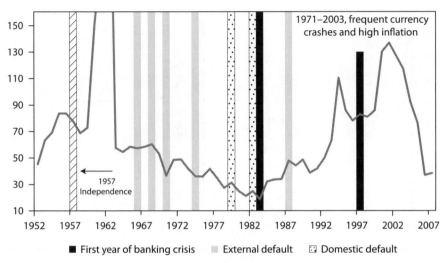

■ First year of banking crisis   ▨ External default   ⊡ Domestic default

Sources: Reinhart and Rogoff (2009) and sources cited therein.

Table 2.25 Ghana: Default, restructuring, banking crises, growth collapses, and IMF programs, 1957–2009

External default/ restructuring	Duration (in years)	Domestic default/ restructuring	Banking crisis dates (first year)	Hyper- inflation dates	Share of years in external default	Share of years in inflation crisis	4 worst output collapses, year (decline)
1966	1	1979	1982	n.a.	9.4	45.3	1955 (6.4)
1968	1	1982	*1997*				1975 (12.5)
1970	1						1982 (6.9)
1974	1						1983 (4.6)
1987	1						
Number of episodes:							
5		2	2	0			

Memorandum item on IMF programs, 1952–2009
Dates of programs   Total
1966–69, 1979, 1983, 1984, 1986, 1987(2), 1988, 1995, 1999, 2003   14

n.a. = not applicable

Note: Banking crisis years shown in *italics* indicate that the episode was not deemed to be a systemic crisis.

Figure 2.26a Greece: Central government (domestic plus external) debt, default, hyperinflation, and banking crises, 1848–2009

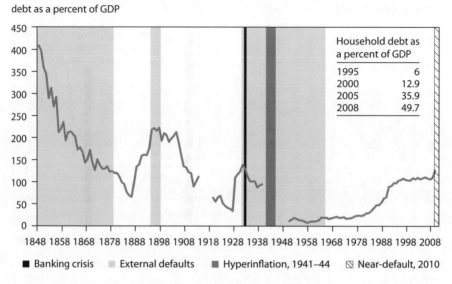

debt as a percent of GDP

	Household debt as a percent of GDP
1995	6
2000	12.9
2005	35.9
2008	49.7

■ Banking crisis　▨ External defaults　■ Hyperinflation, 1941–44　▨ Near-default, 2010

Sources: Lazaretou (2005), Levandis (1944), Reinhart and Rogoff (2009) and sources cited therein.

Table 2.26 Greece: Default, restructuring, banking crises, growth collapses, hyperinflation, and IMF programs, 1829–2009

External default/ restructuring	Duration (in years)	Domestic default/ restructuring	Banking crisis dates (first year)	Hyper-inflation dates	Share of years in external default	Share of years in inflation crisis	5 worst output collapses, year (decline)[1]
1826–42	17	1932–51	1931	1941–44	48.1	12.7	1847 (14.0)
1843–59	17		*1991*				1852 (14.7)
1860–78	19						1856 (11.7)
1894–97	4						1891 (11.5)
1932–64	33						1919 (17.7)
Number of episodes:							
5		1	2	1			

Memorandum item on IMF programs, 1952–2007
Dates of programs　　　　　　　　　　　　　　　　　　　　　　　　　　　Total
None　　　　　　　　　　　　　　　　　　　　　　　　　　　　　　　　　0

1. Excludes World Wars I and II.

Note: Banking crisis years shown in *italics* indicate that the episode was not deemed to be a systemic crisis.

Source: Kostelenos et al. (2007).

Figure 2.26b   Greece: Government domestic debt, default, and banking crises, 1884–1939

loans to the government as a percent of central bank loans

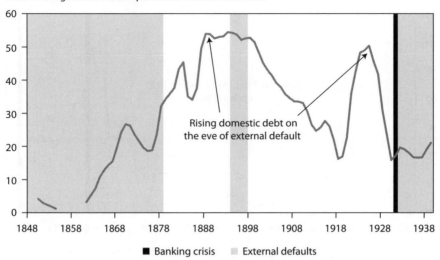

■ Banking crisis   ▨ External defaults

Sources: Lazaretou (2005), Levandis (1944), Reinhart and Rogoff (2009) and sources cited therein.

Figure 2.27 Guatemala: Central government (domestic plus external) debt, default, and devaluation, 1920–2009

debt as a percent of GDP

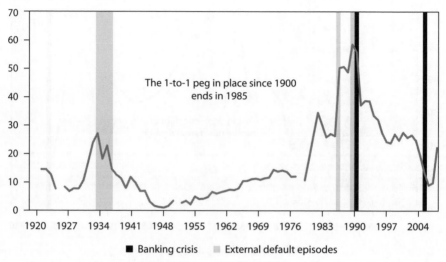

The 1-to-1 peg in place since 1900 ends in 1985

■ Banking crisis ▨ External default episodes

Sources: Reinhart and Rogoff (2009) and sources cited therein.

Table 2.27 Guatemala: Default, restructuring, banking crises, growth collapses, and IMF programs, 1838–2009

External default/ restructuring	Duration (in years)	Domestic default/ restructuring	Banking crisis dates (first year)	Hyper-inflation dates	Share of years in external default	Share of years in inflation crisis	5 worst output collapses, year (decline)
1828–56	29	n.a.	*1991*	n.a.	31.4	3.5	1922 (5.6)
1876–88	13		2001				1931 (6.7)
1894	1		2006				1932 (12.5)
1899–1913	14						1943 (33.3)
1933–36	4						1982 (3.5)
1986	1						
1989	1						
Number of episodes:							
7		0	3	0			

Memorandum item on IMF programs, 1952–2009
Dates of programs
1960–61, 1966–70, 1972, 1981, 1983, 1988, 1992, 2002–03, 2009

Total
15

n.a. = not applicable

Note: Banking crisis years shown in *italics* indicate that the episode was not deemed to be a systemic crisis.

Figure 2.28 Honduras: Central government (domestic plus external) debt, default, and devaluation, 1914–2009

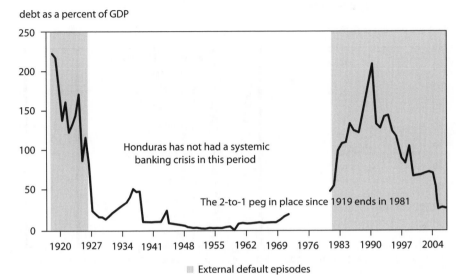

debt as a percent of GDP

Honduras has not had a systemic banking crisis in this period

The 2-to-1 peg in place since 1919 ends in 1981

■ External default episodes

Sources: Reinhart and Rogoff (2009) and sources cited therein.

Table 2.28 Honduras: Default, restructuring, banking crises, growth collapses, and IMF programs, 1838–2009

External default/ restructuring	Duration (in years)	Domestic default/ restructuring	Banking crisis dates (first year)	Hyper-inflation dates	Share of years in external default	Share of years in inflation crisis	5 worst output collapses, year (decline)
1828–67	40	n.a.	1999	n.a.	65.1	3.5	1924 (6.6)
1873–1925	53		2001				1932 (10.4)
1981–2009	29						1933 (6.2)
Number of episodes:							1942 (8.6)
3		0	2	0			1954 (5.7)

Memorandum item on IMF programs, 1952–2009
Dates of programs
1957, 1959–64, 1966, 1968–69, 1971–72, 1979, 1982, 1990,
1992, 1999, 2004, 2008

Total
19

n.a. = not applicable

Figure 2.29 Hungary: Central government (domestic plus external) debt, default, hyperinflation, and banking crises, 1880–2009

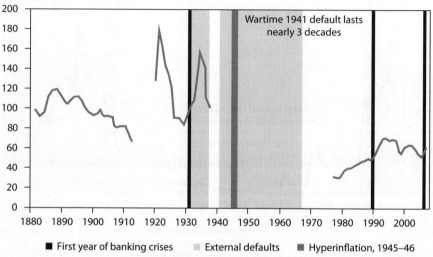

debt as a percent of GDP

Wartime 1941 default lasts nearly 3 decades

■ First year of banking crises   ▨ External defaults   ■ Hyperinflation, 1945–46

Sources: Reinhart and Rogoff (2009) and sources cited therein.

Table 2.29 Hungary: Default, restructuring, banking crises, growth collapses, hyperinflation, and IMF programs, 1918–2009

External default/ restructuring	Duration (in years)	Domestic default/ restructuring	Banking crisis dates (first year)	Hyper-inflation dates	Share of years in external default	Share of years in inflation crisis	4 worst output collapses, year (decline)
1932–37	7	n.a.	1931	1945–46	37	14.1	1931 (4.8)
1941–67	27		1991				1990 (6.7)
			2008				1991 (11.9)
Number of episodes:							*2009 (6.7)*
2		0	3	1			

Memorandum item on IMF programs, 1952–2009
Dates of programs   Total
1982, 1984, 1988, 1990–91, 1993, 1996, 2008   8

n.a. = not applicable

Notes: Summary of private forecasts for 2009 in *italics*.

Figure 2.30a   Iceland: Central government (domestic plus external) debt and banking crises, 1908–2009

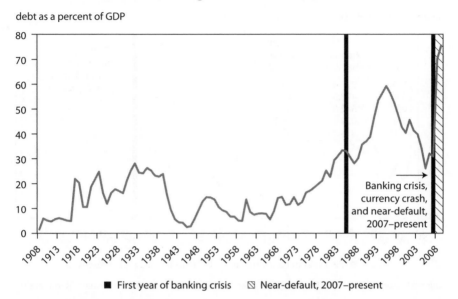

debt as a percent of GDP

Banking crisis, currency crash, and near-default, 2007–present

■ First year of banking crisis   ⊠ Near-default, 2007–present

Sources: Historical Statistics of Iceland, 2010; Reinhart and Rogoff (2009) and sources cited therein.

Table 2.30   Iceland: Default, restructuring, banking crises, growth collapses, and IMF programs, 1918–2009

External default/ restructuring	Duration (in years)	Domestic default/ restructuring	Banking crisis dates (first year)	Hyper- inflation dates	Share of years in external default	Share of years in inflation crisis	5 worst output collapses, year (decline)[1]
n.a.	n.a.	n.a.	*1985*	n.a.	n.a.	25	1916 (11.7)
2007–10	"near" 3		2007				1918 (6.2)
							1920 (15.2)
Number of episodes:							1968 (5.6)
0		0	2	0			*2009 (8.5)*

Memorandum item on IMF programs, 1952–2009
Dates of programs   Total
1960, 2008   2

n.a. = not applicable

1. The reported declines for 1916, 1918, and 1920 are on a per capita basis (Historical Statistics of Iceland, 2010).

Notes: Summary of private forecasts for 2009 in *italics*. Banking crisis years shown in *italics* indicate that the episode was not deemed to be a systemic crisis.

Figure 2.30b   Iceland: External (public plus private) debt and banking crises, 1922–2009

debt as a percent of GDP

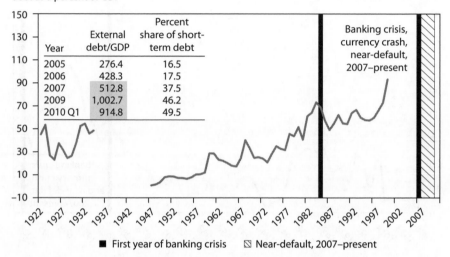

Year	External debt/GDP	Percent share of short-term debt
2005	276.4	16.5
2006	428.3	17.5
2007	512.8	37.5
2009	1,002.7	46.2
2010 Q1	914.8	49.5

Banking crisis, currency crash, near-default, 2007–present

■ First year of banking crisis   ☒ Near-default, 2007–present

Sources: Historical Statistics of Iceland, 2010; Reinhart and Rogoff (2009) and sources cited therein.

Figure 2.30c   Iceland banking survey: Domestic credit and banking crises, 1970–2008

credit outstanding at end of period as a percent of GDP, 4-quarter moving average

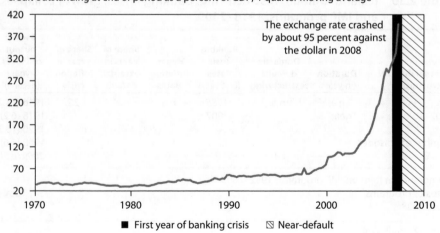

The exchange rate crashed by about 95 percent against the dollar in 2008

■ First year of banking crisis   ☒ Near-default

Notes: For periods where no quarterly nominal GDP is available, a moving-average interpolation method is used.

Sources: International Monetary Fund, *International Financial Statistics;* Reinhart and Rogoff (2009) and sources cited therein.

Figure 2.31   India: Public (domestic plus external) debt reschedulings, near-default, and banking crises, 1835–2009

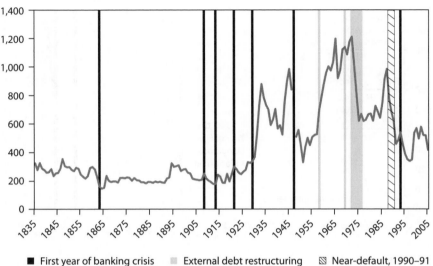

debt as a percent of exports

■ First year of banking crisis   ▨ External debt restructuring   ▨ Near-default, 1990–91

Sources: Reinhart and Rogoff (2009) and sources cited therein.

Table 2.31   India: Default, restructuring, banking crises, growth collapses, and IMF programs, 1835–2009 (calculations since independence—1947, reported)

External default/ restructuring	Duration (in years)	Domestic default/ restructuring	Banking crisis dates (first year)	Hyper-inflation dates	Share of years in external default	Share of years in inflation crisis	5 worst output collapses, year (decline)
1958	1	n.a.	1863	n.a.	11.1	3.2	1891 (9.2)
1969	1		1908				1899 (7.8)
1972–76	5		1914				1918 (12.8)
1989–90			1921				1920 (7.9)
			1929				1947 (17.2)
			1947				
Number of episodes:			1993				
3		0	7	0			

Memorandum item on IMF programs, 1952–2009
Dates of programs   Total
1957, 1962–63, 1965, 1981, 1991 (2)   7

n.a. = not applicable

Notes: Near-default (*italics*) not counted in total.

Figure 2.32a   Indonesia: Central government (domestic plus external) debt, default, and banking crises, 1911–2009

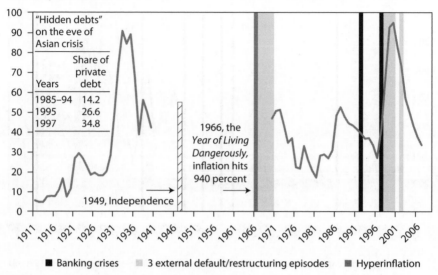

debt as a percent of GDP

"Hidden debts" on the eve of Asian crisis

Years	Share of private debt
1985–94	14.2
1995	26.6
1997	34.8

1966, the *Year of Living Dangerously*, inflation hits 940 percent

1949, Independence

■ Banking crises   ■ 3 external default/restructuring episodes   ■ Hyperinflation

Sources: Creutzberg (1976), Reinhart and Rogoff (2009) and sources cited therein.

Table 2.32   Indonesia: Default, restructuring, banking crises, growth collapses, hyperinflation, and IMF programs, 1800–2009
(calculations since independence—1949, reported)

External default/ restructuring	Duration (in years)	Domestic default/ restructuring	Banking crisis dates (first year)	Hyper- inflation dates	Share of years in external default	Share of years in inflation crisis	5 worst output collapses, year (decline)
1966–70	5	n.a.	1992	1966	14.8	31.1	1931 (7.1)
1998–2000	3		1997				1958 (4.7)
2002	1						1963 (4.2)
							1967 (4.4)
Number of episodes:							1998 (13.1)
3		0	2	1			

Memorandum item on IMF programs, 1952–2009
Dates of programs   Total
1961, 1963, 1968–73, 1997–98, 2000   11

n.a. = not applicable

Figure 2.32b   Indonesia banking survey: Domestic credit, default and banking crises, 1970–2008

credit outstanding at end of period as a percent of GDP, 4-quarter moving average

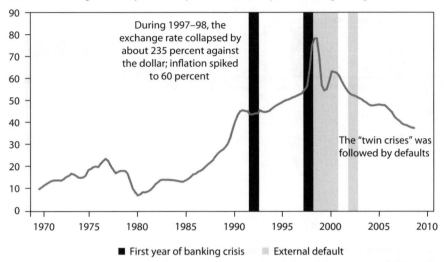

During 1997–98, the exchange rate collapsed by about 235 percent against the dollar; inflation spiked to 60 percent

The "twin crises" was followed by defaults

■ First year of banking crisis   ▨ External default

Notes: For periods where no quarterly nominal GDP is available, a moving-average interpolation method is used.

Sources: International Monetary Fund, *International Financial Statistics;* Reinhart and Rogoff (2009) and sources cited therein.

Figure 2.33a   Ireland: Central government (domestic plus external) debt and banking crises, 1929–2009

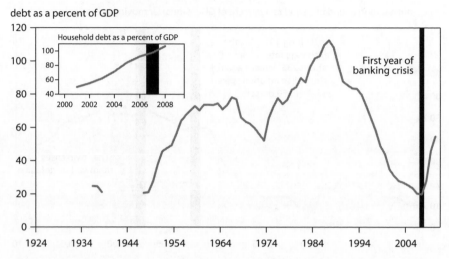

Sources: National Treasury Management Agency (2010); Reinhart and Rogoff (2009) and sources cited therein.

Figure 2.33   Ireland: Default, restructuring, banking crises, growth collapses, and IMF programs, 1919–2009

External default/ restructuring	Duration (in years)	Domestic default/ restructuring	Banking crisis dates (first year)	Hyper-inflation dates	Share of years in external default	Share of years in inflation crisis	5 worst output collapses, year (decline)
n.a.	n.a.		1836	n.a.	n.a.		1933 (2.5)
			1856				1937 (3.8)
							1958 (2.1)
			2007				2008 (3.0)
Number of episodes:							*2009 (7.5)*
0		0	3	0			

Memorandum item on IMF programs, 1952–2009	
Dates of programs	Total
None	0

n.a. = not applicable

Notes: Summary of private forecasts for 2009 in *italics*.

Figure 2.33b   Ireland banking survey: Domestic credit and banking crises, 1970–2010Q2

credit outstanding at end of period as a percent of GDP, 4-quarter moving average

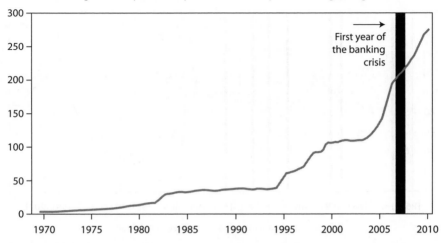

Notes: For periods where no quarterly nominal GDP is available, a moving-average interpolation method is used.

Sources: International Monetary Fund, *International Financial Statistics;* Reinhart and Rogoff (2009) and sources cited therein.

Figure 2.34   Italy: Central government (domestic plus external) debt, default, and banking crises, 1861–2009

debt as a percent of GDP

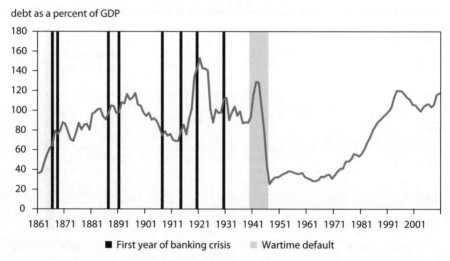

■ First year of banking crisis   ▨ Wartime default

Sources: Francese and Pace (2008), Reinhart and Rogoff (2009) and sources cited therein.

Table 2.34   Italy: Default, restructuring, banking crises, growth collapses, and IMF programs, 1800–2009

External default/ restructuring	Duration (in years)	Domestic default/ restructuring	Banking crisis dates (first year)	Hyper-inflation dates	Share of years in external default	Share of years in inflation crisis	7 worst output collapses, year (decline)
1940–46	7	n.a.	1866	1944	3.3	10.5	1867 (8.3)
			1887				1881 (6.7)
			1891				1892 (5.6)
			1893				1919 (16.7)
			1907				1920 (8.7)
			1914				1930 (4.9)
			1921				*2009 (4.8)*
			1930				
			1935				
			1990				
			2008				
Number of episodes:							
1		0	11	0			

Memorandum item on IMF programs, 1952–2009
Dates of programs   Total
1974, 1977   2

n.a. = not applicable

Notes: Summary of private forecasts for 2009 in *italics*. Banking crisis years shown in *italics* indicate that the episode was not deemed to be a systemic crisis.

Figure 2.35a   Japan: Central government (domestic plus external) debt, default, and banking crises, 1885–2009

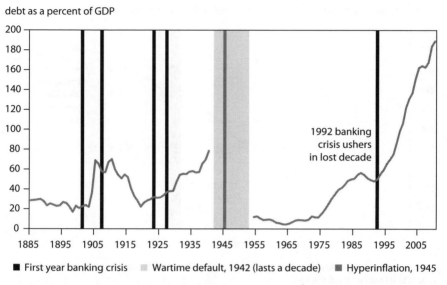

debt as a percent of GDP

■ First year banking crisis   ▨ Wartime default, 1942 (lasts a decade)   ▨ Hyperinflation, 1945

Sources: Reinhart and Rogoff (2009) and sources cited therein.

Table 2.35   Japan: Default, restructuring, banking crises, growth collapses, hyperinflation, and IMF programs, 1800–2009

External default/ restructuring	Duration (in years)	Domestic default/ restructuring	Banking crisis dates (first year)	Hyper- inflation dates	Share of years in external default	Share of years in inflation crisis	5 worst output collapses, year (decline)
1942–52	11	1946–48	1872	1945	5.2	11	1896 (5.5)
			1882				1899 (7.4)
			1901				1920 (6.2)
			1907				1930 (7.3)
			1917				*2009 (5.0)*
			1923				
			1927				
			1992				
Number of episodes:							
1		1	8	1			

Memorandum item on IMF programs, 1952–2009	
Dates of programs	Total
1962, 1964	2

Notes: Summary of private forecasts for 2009 in *italics*.

Figure 2.35b   Japan banking survey: Domestic credit and banking crises, 1970–2008

credit outstanding at end of period as a percent of GDP, 4-quarter moving average

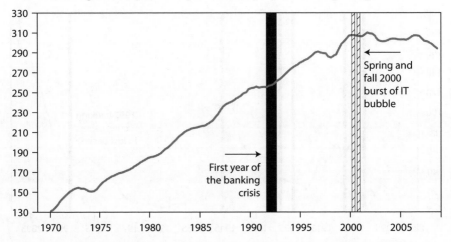

Sources: International Monetary Fund, *International Financial Statistics;* Reinhart and Rogoff (2009) and sources cited therein.

Figure 2.36   Kenya: External (public plus private) debt, default, and banking crises, 1970–2009

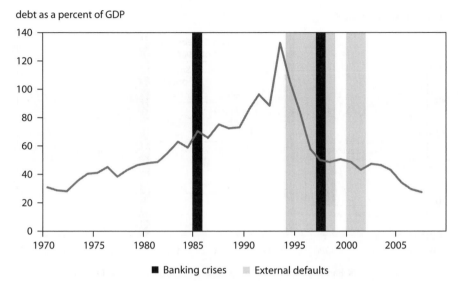

debt as a percent of GDP

■ Banking crises   ▨ External defaults

Sources: Reinhart and Rogoff (2009) and sources cited therein.

Table 2.36   Kenya: Default, restructuring, banking crises, growth collapses, and IMF programs, 1963–2009

External default/ restructuring	Duration (in years)	Domestic default/ restructuring	Banking crisis dates (first year)	Hyper- inflation dates	Share of years in external default	Share of years in inflation crisis	3 worst output collapses, year (decline)[1]
1994–98	5	n.a.	1985	n.a.	14.9	8.5	1952 (11.1)
2000–01	2		1996				1953 (2.5)
							1961 (2.4)
Number of episodes:							
2		0	2	0			

Memorandum item on IMF programs, 1952–2009
Dates of programs   Total
1975, 1977–80, 1982–83, 1985, 1988(2), 1989, 1993, 1996, 2000, 2003   15

n.a. = not applicable

Figure 2.37a   Korea: External (public plus private) debt, near-default, and banking crises, 1970–2009

debt as a percent of GDP

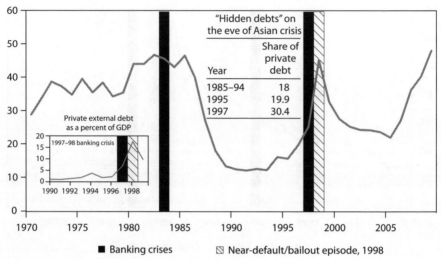

■ Banking crises   ⧄ Near-default/bailout episode, 1998

Sources: Reinhart and Rogoff (2009) and sources cited therein.

Table 2.37   Korea: Default, restructuring, banking crises, growth collapses, and IMF programs, 1945–2009

External default/ restructuring	Duration (in years)	Domestic default/ restructuring	Banking crisis dates (first year)	Hyper- inflation dates	Share of years in external default	Share of years in inflation crisis	5 worst output collapses, year (decline)
1997–98	2		1983	n.a.	0	15.4	1920 (12.3)
			1985				1922 (7.1)
			1997				1939 (10.4)
							1951 (7.7)
Number of episodes:							1998 (6.9)
0		0	3	0			

Memorandum item on IMF programs, 1952–2009
Dates of programs   Total
1965–75, 1977, 1980–81, 1983, 1985, 1997   17

n.a. = not applicable

Notes: Near default (*italics*) not counted in total.

Sources: Pre-World War II real GDP: Bassino and van del Eng (2006).

Figure 2.37b   Korea banking survey: Domestic credit and banking crises, 1970–2008

credit outstanding at end of period as a percent of GDP

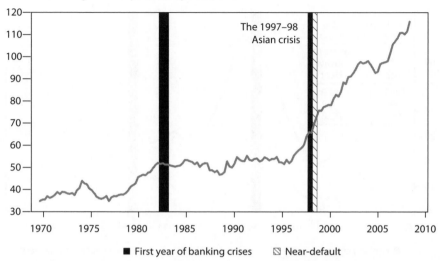

■ First year of banking crises   ▨ Near-default

Sources: International Monetary Fund, *International Financial Statistics*; Reinhart and Rogoff (2009) and sources cited therein.

Figure 2.38a Malaysia: External (public plus private) debt, near-default, and banking crises, 1970–2009

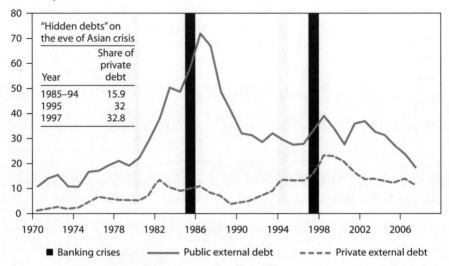

debt as a percent of GDP

"Hidden debts" on the eve of Asian crisis

Year	Share of private debt
1985–94	15.9
1995	32
1997	32.8

■ Banking crises ── Public external debt ---- Private external debt

Sources: Reinhart and Rogoff (2009) and sources cited therein.

Table 2.38 Malaysia: Default, restructuring, banking crises, growth collapses, and IMF programs, 1963–2009

External default/ restructuring	Duration (in years)	Domestic default/ restructuring	Banking crisis dates (first year)	Hyper-inflation dates	Share of years in external default	Share of years in inflation crisis	5 worst output collapses, year (decline)
n.a.	n.a.	n.a.	1985 1997	n.a.	0	0	1912 (7.2) 1925 (12.4) 1938 (4.9) 1951 (5.5) 1998 (7.4)
Number of episodes: 0		0	2	0			

Memorandum item on IMF programs, 1952–2009	
Dates of programs	Total
None	0

n.a. = not applicable

Sources: Pre-World War II real GDP: Bassino and van del Eng (2006).

Figure 2.38b   Malaysia banking survey: Domestic credit, default and banking crises, 1970–2008

credit outstanding at end of period as a percent of GDP, 4-quarter moving average

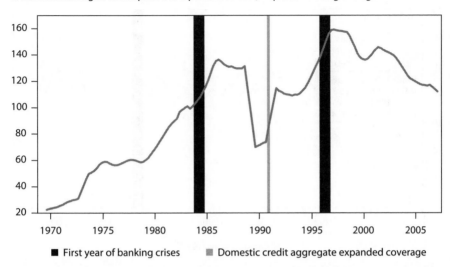

- First year of banking crises   Domestic credit aggregate expanded coverage

Notes: For periods where no quarterly nominal GDP is available, a moving-average interpolation method is used.

Sources: International Monetary Fund, *International Financial Statistics;* Reinhart and Rogoff (2009) and sources cited therein.

Figure 2.39 Mauritius: External (public plus private) debt, default, and banking crises, 1970–2009

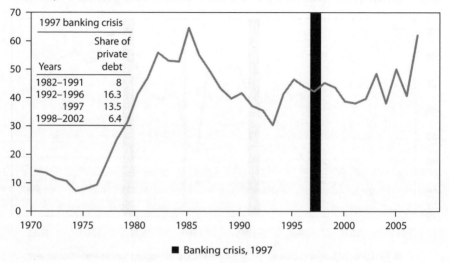

debt as a percent of GDP

	1997 banking crisis	
		Share of private debt
	Years	debt
	1982–1991	8
	1992–1996	16.3
	1997	13.5
	1998–2002	6.4

■ Banking crisis, 1997

Sources: Reinhart and Rogoff (2009) and sources cited therein.

Table 2.39 Mauritius: Default, restructuring, banking crises, growth collapses, and IMF programs, 1968–2009

External default/ restructuring	Duration (in years)	Domestic default/ restructuring	Banking crisis dates (first year)	Hyper-inflation dates	Share of years in external default	Share of years in inflation crisis	3 worst output collapses, year (decline)
n.a.	n.a.	n.a.	*1997*	n.a.	0	11.9	1964 (6.9)
							1968 (6.9)
Number of episodes:							1980 (10.1)
0		0	1	0			

Memorandum item on IMF programs, 1952–2009
Dates of programs   Total
1978–81, 1983, 1985   6

n.a. = not applicable

Note: Banking crisis years shown in *italics* indicate that the episode was not deemed to be a systemic crisis.

Figure 2.40a Mexico: Public foreign bond issues, default, and banking crises, 1824–1914

billions of US dollars, three-year sum

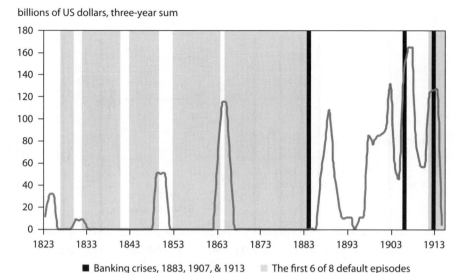

■ Banking crises, 1883, 1907, & 1913   ▨ The first 6 of 8 default episodes

Sources: Reinhart and Rogoff (2009) and sources cited therein.

Table 2.40 Mexico: Default, restructuring, banking crises, growth collapses, and IMF programs, 1821–2009

External default/ restructuring	Duration (in years)	Domestic default/ restructuring	Banking crisis dates (first year)	Hyper-inflation dates	Share of years in external default	Share of years in inflation crisis	6 worst output collapses, year (decline)
1828–30	3	1850	1883	n.a.	43.9	11.1	1902 (7.1)
1833–41	1	1928–32	1907				1930 (6.3)
1844–50	7	1982	1913				1932 (15.0)
1854–64	11		1920				1983 (4.3)
1866–85	20		1929				1995 (6.2)
1914–22	9		1981				*2009 (6.7)*
1928–42	15		1994				
1982–90	9						
1994–95							
Number of episodes:							
8		3	7	0			

Memorandum item on IMF programs, 1952–2009
Dates of programs   Total
1954, 1959, 1961, 1977, 1983, 1986, 1989, 1995, 1999   9

n.a. = not applicable

Notes: Near defaults (not counted in total) are in *italics*. Summary of private forecasts for 2009 in *italics*.

Figure 2.40b Mexico: Central government (domestic plus external) debt, default, and banking crises, 1872–2009

debt as a percent of GDP

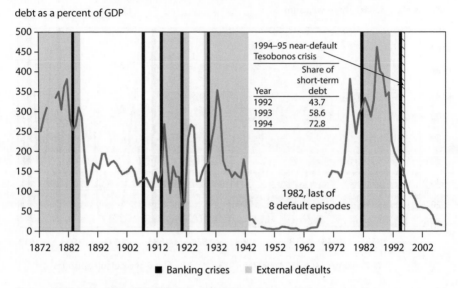

■ Banking crises   ▨ External defaults

Sources: Reinhart and Rogoff (2009) and sources cited therein.

**Figure 2.41 Morocco: External (public plus private) debt, default, and
banking crises, 1970–2009**

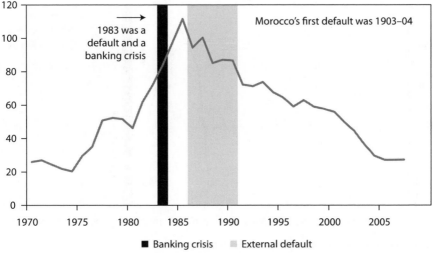

debt as a percent of GDP

Sources: Reinhart and Rogoff (2009) and sources cited therein.

**Table 2.41 Morocco: Default, restructuring, banking crises, growth
collapses, and IMF programs, 1956–2009**

External default/ restructuring	Duration (in years)	Domestic default/ restructuring	Banking crisis dates (first year)	Hyper- inflation dates	Share of years in external default	Share of years in inflation crisis	3 worst output collapses, year (decline)
1903–04	2	n.a.	1983	n.a.	11.1	0	1981 (2.8)
1983	1						1992 (4.0)
1986–90	5						1995 (6.6)
Number of episodes:							
3		0	1	0			

Memorandum item on IMF programs, 1952–2009
Dates of programs   Total
1959, 1965–69, 1971, 1980–83, 1985–86, 1988, 1990, 1992   16

n.a. = not applicable

Figure 2.42   Myanmar: External (public plus private) debt, default, and banking crises, 1970–2009

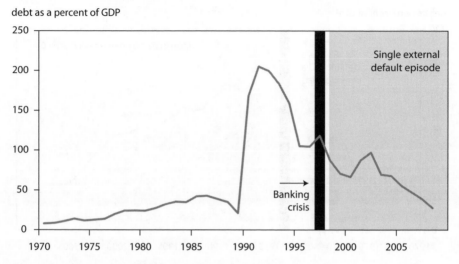

debt as a percent of GDP

Sources: Reinhart and Rogoff (2009) and sources cited therein.

Table 2.42   Myanmar: Default, restructuring, banking crises, growth collapses, and IMF programs, 1948–2009

External default/ restructuring	Duration (in years)	Domestic default/ restructuring	Banking crisis dates (first year)	Hyper- inflation dates	Share of years in external default	Share of years in inflation crisis	4 worst output collapses, year (decline)
1997–2009	13	1984 1987	1996	n.a.	21	37.1	1954 (6.2) 1966 (4.2) 1987 (4.0) 1988 (11.4)
Number of episodes: 1		2	4	0			

Memorandum item on IMF programs, 1952–2009
Dates of programs   Total
1969, 1973–74, 1977–78, 1981   6

n.a. = not applicable

Figure 2.43 Netherlands: General government (domestic plus external) and banking crises, 1812–2009

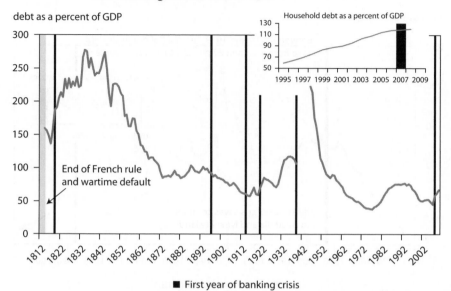

■ First year of banking crisis

Sources: Bos (2007), Reinhart and Rogoff (2009), and sources cited therein.

Table 2.43 Netherlands: Default, restructuring, banking crises, growth collapses, and IMF programs, 1800–2009

External default/ restructuring	Duration (in years)	Domestic default/ restructuring	Banking crisis dates (first year)	Hyper- inflation dates	Share of years in external default	Share of years in inflation crisis	4 worst output collapses, year (decline)[1]
1802–14	13	1802–14	1819	n.a.	6.2	0	1830 (3.5)
			1897				1896 (3.8)
			1914				1931 (6.1)
			1921				*2009 (4.0)*
			1939				
			2008				
Number of episodes:							
1		1	6	0			

Memorandum item on IMF programs, 1952–2009	
Dates of programs	Total
1957	1

n.a. = not applicable

1. Excludes World Wars I and II.

Notes: Summary of private forecasts for 2009 in *italics*.

Figure 2.44a   New Zealand: Central government (domestic plus external) debt and banking crises, 1860–2009

debt as a percent of GDP

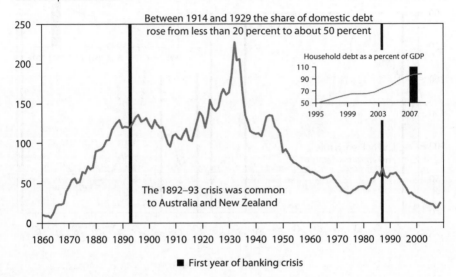

■ First year of banking crisis

Sources: Reinhart and Rogoff (2009) and sources cited therein.

Table 2.44   New Zealand: Default, restructuring, banking crises, growth collapses, and IMF programs, 1907–2009

External default/ restructuring	Duration (in years)	Domestic default/ restructuring	Banking crisis dates (first year)	Hyper-inflation dates	Share of years in external default	Share of years in inflation crisis	5 worst output collapses, year (decline)[1]
n.a.	n.a.	n.a.	1893		0	0	1876 (11.6)
			1987				1908 (6.9)
							1931 (8.5)
							1948 (9.9)
Number of episodes:							1951 (7.6)
0		0	2	0			

Memorandum item on IMF programs, 1952–2009
Dates of programs   Total
1967   1

n.a. = not applicable

1. Excludes World Wars I and II.

Note: Banking crisis years shown in *italics* indicate that the episode was not deemed to be a systemic crisis.

**Figure 2.44b   New Zealand: Private capital inflows from the United
Kingdom and banking crises, 1865–1905**

capital flows as a percent of exports

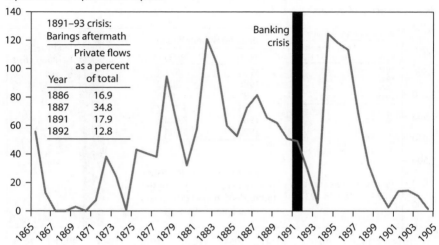

Sources: Stone (1999), Reinhart and Rogoff (2009), and sources cited therein.

Figure 2.45 Nicaragua: Central government (domestic plus external) debt and default, hyperinflation, and banking crises, 1914–2009

debt as a percent of exports

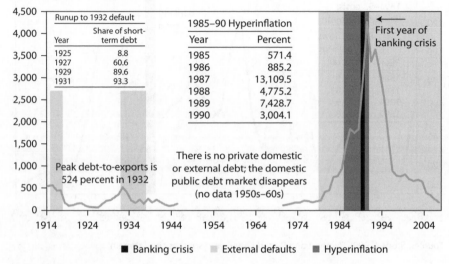

Notes: No GDP data are available prior to 1950; hence we scale debt by exports.

Sources: Reinhart and Rogoff (2009) and sources cited therein.

Table 2.45 Nicaragua: Default, restructuring, banking crises, growth collapses, hyperinflation, and IMF programs, 1838–2009

External default/ restructuring	Duration (in years)	Domestic default/ restructuring	Banking crisis dates (first year)	Hyper- inflation dates	Share of years in external default	Share of years in inflation crisis	5 worst output collapses, year (decline)
1828–74	47	1985–90	1987	1985–90	47.1	12.2	1930 (19.2)
1894–95	2		*2000*				1936 (20.4)
							1978 (7.9)
1911–12	2						1979 (26.6)
1915–17	3						1988 (12.4)
1932–37	6						
1979–2009	31						
Number of episodes:							
6		1	2	1			

Memorandum item on IMF programs, 1952–2009

Dates of programs	Total
1956–58, 1960, 1963–64, 1968–70, 1972, 1979, 1991, 1994, 1998, 2002	15

Note: Banking crisis years shown in *italics* indicate that the episode was not deemed to be a systemic crisis.

Figure 2.46   Nigeria: External (public plus private) debt, default, and banking crises, 1970–2009

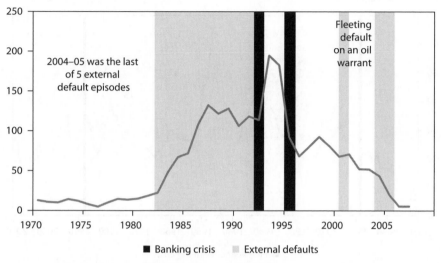

debt as a percent of GDP

Sources: Reinhart and Rogoff (2009) and sources cited therein.

Table 2.46   Nigeria: Default, restructuring, banking crises, growth collapses, and IMF programs, 1960–2009

External default/ restructuring	Duration (in years)	Domestic default/ restructuring	Banking crisis dates (first year)	Hyper-inflation dates	Share of years in external default	Share of years in inflation crisis	5 worst output collapses, year (decline)
1982–92	11	n.a.	1992	n.a.	28	24	1967 (15.5)
1986–88	3		1995				1978 (5.9)
1992	1						1983 (5.1)
2001	1						1986 (8.8)
2004–05	2						1987 (10.8)
Number of episodes:							
5		0	2	0			

Memorandum item on IMF programs, 1952–2009
Dates of programs   Total
1987, 1989, 1991, 2000   4

n.a. = not applicable

Figure 2.47a   Norway: Central government (domestic plus external) debt and banking crises, 1880–2009

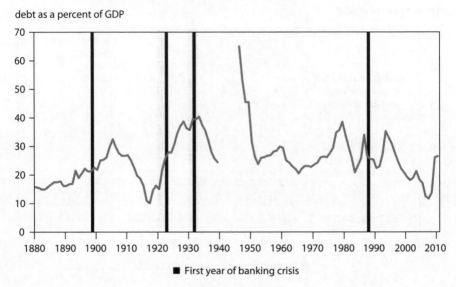

debt as a percent of GDP

■ First year of banking crisis

Sources: Reinhart and Rogoff (2009) and sources cited therein.

Table 2.47   Norway: Default, restructuring, banking crises, growth collapses, and IMF programs, 1800–2009

External default/ restructuring	Duration (in years)	Domestic default/ restructuring	Banking crisis dates (first year)	Hyper- inflation dates	Share of years in external default	Share of years in inflation crisis	4 worst output collapses, year (decline)
n.a.	n.a.	n.a.	1898	n.a.	n.a.	5.2	1831 (7.0)
			1921				1848 (4.7)
			1931				1921 (9.7)
			1936				1931 (7.8)
			1987				
Number of episodes:							
0		0	5	0			

Memorandum item on IMF programs, 1952–2009
Dates of programs   Total
None   0

n.a. = not applicable

Figure 2.47b   Norway: Domestic private credit, 1900–2004

amount outstanding at year-end as a percent of GDP

■ First year of banking crises

Sources: Eitrheim, Gerdrup, and Klovland (2004), Reinhart and Rogoff (2009) and sources cited therein.

Figure 2.48   Panama: Central government (domestic plus external) debt and banking crises, 1914–2009

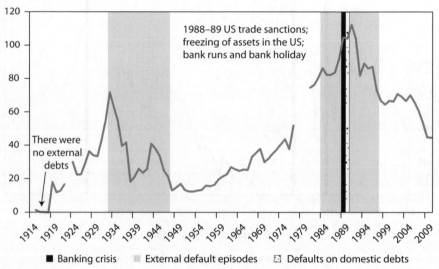

debt as a percent of GDP

1988–89 US trade sanctions; freezing of assets in the US; bank runs and bank holiday

There were no external debts

■ Banking crisis   ▨ External default episodes   ⊡ Defaults on domestic debts

Notes: No GDP data are available prior to 1945; hence, we scale debt by exports and adjust it by the ratio of exports to GDP to splice the pre–World War II series.

Sources: Reinhart and Rogoff (2009) and sources cited therein.

Table 2.48   Panama: Default, restructuring, banking crises, growth collapses, and IMF programs, 1903–2009

External default/ restructuring	Duration (in years)	Domestic default/ restructuring	Banking crisis dates (first year)	Hyper- inflation dates	Share of years in external default	Share of years in inflation crisis	3 worst output collapses, year (decline)
1932–46	15	88–89	1988	n.a.	27.1	0	1948 (5.9)
1983–96	14						1983 (4.5)
1987–94							1988 (13.5)
Number of episodes:							
3		1	1	0			

Memorandum item on IMF programs, 1952–2009
Dates of programs   Total
1965, 1968–75, 1977–80, 1982–83, 1985, 1992, 1995, 1997, 2000   20

n.a. = not applicable

Notes: The 1987–94 default was on bonds, while the 1983–96 episode was on bank loans.

Figure 2.49 **Paraguay: External (public plus private) debt, near-default, and banking crises, 1970–2009**

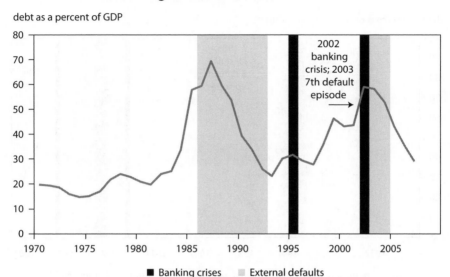

debt as a percent of GDP

2002 banking crisis; 2003 7th default episode →

■ Banking crises   ▨ External defaults

Sources: Reinhart and Rogoff (2009) and sources cited therein.

Table 2.49 **Paraguay: Default, restructuring, banking crises, growth collapses, and IMF programs, 1811–2009**

External default/ restructuring	Duration (in years)	Domestic default/ restructuring	Banking crisis dates (first year)	Hyper- inflation dates	Share of years in external default	Share of years in inflation crisis	4 worst output collapses, year (decline)
1874–85	12	n.a.	1890	n.a.	22.6	11.1	1940 (5.3)
1892–95	4		1997				1947 (13.1)
1920–24	5		2002				1983 (3.0)
1932–44	13						*2009 (4.5)*
1968–69	2						
1986–92	7						
2003–04	2						
Number of episodes:							
7		0	3	0			

Memorandum item on IMF programs, 1952–2009
Dates of programs   Total
1957–61, 1964, 1966, 1968–69, 2003   10

n.a. = not applicable

Notes: Summary of private forecasts for 2009 in *italics*.

Figure 2.50a Peru: Central government (domestic plus external) debt, default, and banking crises, 1917–2009

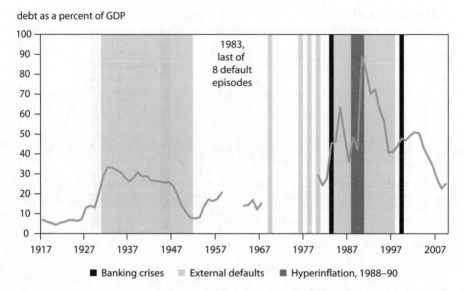

debt as a percent of GDP

1983, last of 8 default episodes

■ Banking crises   ■ External defaults   ■ Hyperinflation, 1988–90

Sources: Reinhart and Rogoff (2009) and sources cited therein.

Table 2.50 Peru: Default, restructuring, banking crises, growth collapses, hyperinflation, and IMF programs, 1821–2009

External default/ restructuring	Duration (in years)	Domestic default/ restructuring	Banking crisis dates (first year)	Hyper-inflation dates	Share of years in external default	Share of years in inflation crisis	5 worst output collapses, year (decline)
1826–48	23	1931–38	1872	1988–90	40.2	13.2	1930 (11.5)
1876–89	14	1985–87	1983				1931 (8.1)
1931–51	21		1999				1983 (9.3)
1969–69	2						1988 (9.4)
1976	1						1989 (13.4)
1978	1						
1980	1						
1984–97	14						
Number of episodes:							
8		2	3	1			

Memorandum item on IMF programs, 1952–2009
Dates of programs
1954, 1958–68, 1970, 1977–79, 1982, 1984, 1993, 1996, 1999,
2001–02, 2004

Total number of years
24

**Figure 2.50b   Peru: Total (public and private) capital inflows from the
United Kingdom and banking crises, 1865–1905**

capital flows as a percent of exports

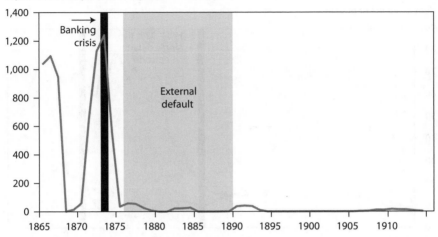

Sources: Stone (1999), Reinhart and Rogoff (2009) and sources cited therein.

Figure 2.51a Philippines: External private and public (domestic plus external) debt, near-default, and banking crises, 1948–2009

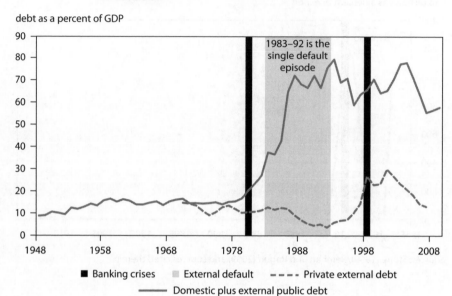

debt as a percent of GDP

1983–92 is the single default episode

■ Banking crises   ▨ External default   – – – – Private external debt
———— Domestic plus external public debt

Sources: Reinhart and Rogoff (2009) and sources cited therein.

Table 2.51 Philippines: Default, restructuring, banking crises, growth collapses, and IMF programs, 1946–2009

External default/ restructuring	Duration (in years)	Domestic default/ restructuring	Banking crisis dates (first year)	Hyper- inflation dates	Share of years in external default	Share of years in inflation crisis	5 worst output collapses, year (decline)
1983–92	10	n.a.	1981 1997	n.a.	18.8	6.3	1904 (13.9) 1923 (6.1) 1935 (6.8) 1984 (7.5)
Number of episodes:							1985 (7.5)
1		0	2	0			

Memorandum item on IMF programs, 1952–2007
Dates of programs   Total
1962–68, 1970–76, 1979–80, 1983–84, 1986, 1989, 1991, 1994, 1998   23

n.a. = not applicable

Sources: Pre-World War II real GDP: Bassino and van del Eng (2006).

Figure 2.51b   Philippines banking survey: Domestic credit, default, and banking crises, 1980–2008

credit outstanding at end of period as a percent of GDP, 4-quarter moving average

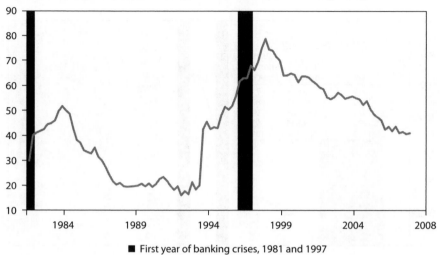

■ First year of banking crises, 1981 and 1997

Notes: For periods where no quarterly nominal GDP is available, a moving-average interpolation method is used.

Sources: International Monetary Fund, *International Financial Statistics;* Reinhart and Rogoff (2009) and sources cited therein.

Figure 2.52a Poland: Central government (domestic plus external) debt, default, hyperinflation, and banking crises, 1917–47

debt as a percent of GDP

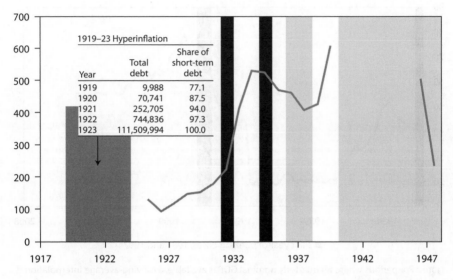

■ First year of banking crises ■ Hyperinflation, 1919–23 ▨ Depression and wartime defaults

Sources: Reinhart and Rogoff (2009) and sources cited therein.

Table 2.52 Poland: Default, restructuring, banking crises, growth collapses, hyperinflation, and IMF programs, 1918–2009

External default/ restructuring	Duration (in years)	Domestic default/ restructuring	Banking crisis dates (first year)	Hyper-inflation dates	Share of years in external default	Share of years in inflation crisis	4 worst output collapses, year (decline)
1936–37	2	n.a.	1931	1919–23	31.5	18.5	1980 (–6.0)
1940–52	13		1934	1990			1981 (10.0)
1981–94	14		1991				1990 (7.2)
							1991 (7.0)
Number of episodes:							
3		0	3	1			

Memorandum item on IMF programs, 1952–2009
Dates of programs   Total number of years
1990–91, 1993–94   4

n.a. = not applicable

Figure 2.52b Poland: Central government (domestic plus external) debt, default, hyperinflation and banking crises, 1984–2009

debt as a percent of GDP

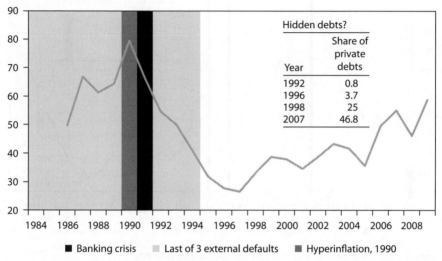

Hidden debts?	
Year	Share of private debts
1992	0.8
1996	3.7
1998	25
2007	46.8

■ Banking crisis   ■ Last of 3 external defaults   ■ Hyperinflation, 1990

Sources: Reinhart and Rogoff (2009) and sources cited therein.

Figure 2.53   Portugal: Central government (domestic plus external) debt, default, and banking crises, 1851–2009

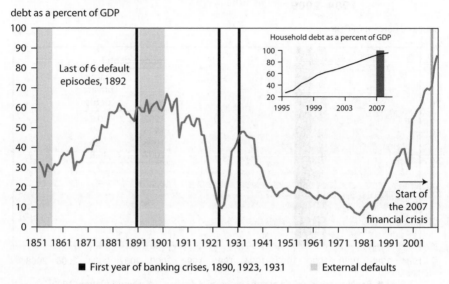

Sources: OECD, Reinhart and Rogoff (2009) and sources cited therein.

Table 2.53   Portugal: Default, restructuring, banking crises, growth collapses, and IMF programs, 1800–2009

External default/ restructuring	Duration (in years)	Domestic default/ restructuring	Banking crisis dates (first year)	Hyper- inflation dates	Share of years in external default	Share of years in inflation crisis	5 worst output collapses, year (decline)
1828	1	n.a.	1828	n.a.	11	9.5	1918 (5.1)
1837–41	5		1846				1928 (9.7)
1850–56	7		1890				1935 (5.3)
1892–01	10		1920				1936 (7.6)
			1923				1940 (6.5)
			1931				
Number of episodes:							
6		0	6	0			

Memorandum item on IMF programs, 1952–2009
Dates of programs   Total number of years
1977, 1978, 1983   3

n.a. = not applicable

Note: Some external default episodes involve two defaults.

Figure 2.54 Romania: External (public plus private) debt, default, and banking crises, 1970–2009

debt as a percent of exports

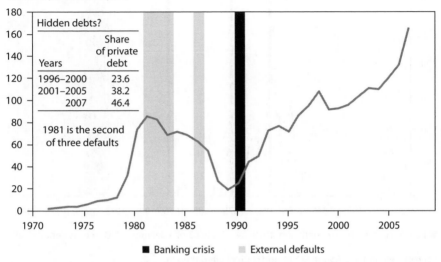

■ Banking crisis ▨ External defaults

Sources: Reinhart and Rogoff (2009) and sources cited therein.

Table 2.54 Romania: Default, restructuring, banking crises, growth collapses, and IMF programs, 1878–2009

External default/ restructuring	Duration (in years)	Domestic default/ restructuring	Banking crisis dates (first year)	Hyper-inflation dates	Share of years in external default	Share of years in inflation crisis	5 worst output collapses, year (decline)
1933–58	26	1933–58	1931	n.a.	22.6	9.8	1989 (5.8)
1981–83	4		1990				1990 (5.6)
1986	1						1991 (12.9)
							1997 (6.1)
Number of episodes:							*2009 (7.2)*
3		1	2	0			

Memorandum item on IMF programs, 1952–2009
Dates of programs   Total number of years
1975, 1977, 1981, 1991–92, 1994, 1997, 1999, 2001, 2004, 2009   10

n.a. = not applicable

Notes: Summary of private forecasts for 2009 in *italics*.

Figure 2.55a Russia: Public foreign bond issues and default, 1815–1945

as a percent of exports

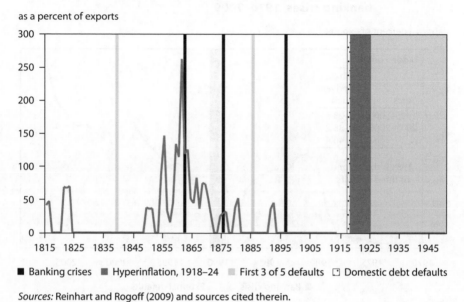

■ Banking crises ■ Hyperinflation, 1918–24 ▨ First 3 of 5 defaults ⬚ Domestic debt defaults

Sources: Reinhart and Rogoff (2009) and sources cited therein.

Table 2.55 Russia: Default, restructuring, banking crises, growth collapses, hyperinflation, and IMF programs, 1800–2009

External default/ restructuring	Duration (in years)	Domestic default/ restructuring	Banking crisis dates (first year)	Hyper- inflation dates	Share of years in external default	Share of years in inflation crisis	5 worst output collapses, year (decline)
1839	1	1917–18	1862	1918–24	38.8	13.8	1992 (14.5)
1885	1	1947	1875	1993			1993 (8.7)
1918–86	69	1957	1896				1994 (12.7)
1991–97	7	1998–99	*1995*				1998 (5.3)
1998–2000	3		1998				*2009 (7.9)*
			2008				
Number of episodes:							
5		4	6	2			

Memorandum item on IMF programs, 1952–2009
Dates of programs   Total number of years
1992, 1995–96, 1999   4

Notes: Summary of private forecasts for 2009 in *italics*. Banking crisis years shown in *italics* indicate that the episode was not deemed to be a systemic crisis.

Figure 2.55b   Russia: External (public plus private) debt, default, hyperinflation, and banking crises, 1985–2009

debt as a percent of GDP

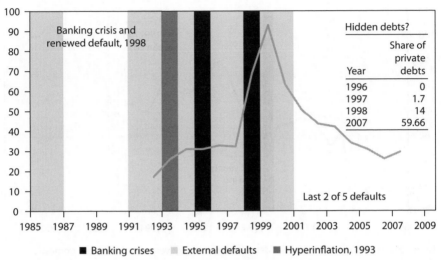

Banking crisis and renewed default, 1998

Hidden debts?

Year	Share of private debts
1996	0
1997	1.7
1998	14
2007	59.66

Last 2 of 5 defaults

■ Banking crises   ▦ External defaults   ■ Hyperinflation, 1993

Sources: Reinhart and Rogoff (2009) and sources cited therein.

Figure 2.56 Singapore: Central government (domestic and external) debt, default, and banking crises, 1969–2009

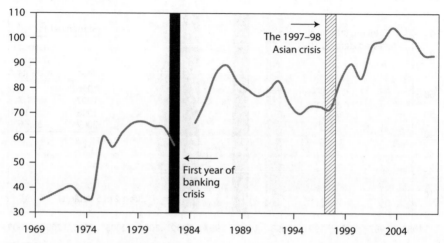

debt as a percent of GDP

The 1997–98 Asian crisis

First year of banking crisis

Notes: Since the mid-1990s all public debts of the central government have been domestic.

Sources: Reinhart and Rogoff (2009) and sources cited therein.

Table 2.56 Singapore: Default, restructuring, banking crises, growth collapses, and IMF programs, 1965–2009

External default/ restructuring	Duration (in years)	Domestic default/ restructuring	Banking crisis dates (first year)	Hyper-inflation dates	Share of years in external default	Share of years in inflation crisis	3 worst output collapses, year (decline)
n.a.	n.a.	n.a.	1982	n.a.	0	2.2	1964 (3.5)
							2001 (2.4)
Number of episodes:							*2009 (2.0)*
0		0	1	0			

Memorandum item on IMF programs, 1952–2009	
Dates of programs	Total number of years
None	0

n.a. = not applicable

Notes: Summary of private forecasts for 2009 in *italics*.

Figure 2.57a   South Africa: Central government (domestic plus external) debt, default, and banking crises, 1911–2009

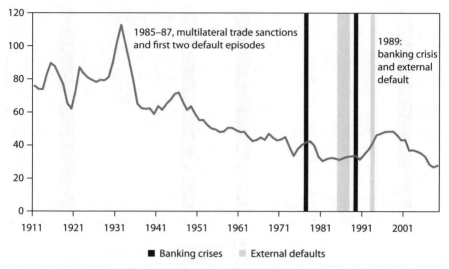

debt as a percent of GDP

1985–87, multilateral trade sanctions and first two default episodes

1989: banking crisis and external default

■ Banking crises   ▨ External defaults

Sources: Reinhart and Rogoff (2009) and sources cited therein.

Table 2.57   South Africa: Default, restructuring, banking crises, growth collapses, and IMF programs, 1800–2009 (calculations since independence—1910, reported)

External default/ restructuring	Duration (in years)	Domestic default/ restructuring	Banking crisis dates (first year)	Hyper-inflation dates	Share of years in external default	Share of years in inflation crisis	3 worst output collapses, year (decline)
1985–87	3	n.a.	1865	n.a.	5	1	1983 (1.8)
1989	1		1877				1992 (2.1)
1993	1		1890				*2009 (1.8)*
			1977				
Number of episodes:			*1989*				
3		0	5	0			

Memorandum item on IMF programs, 1952–2009	
Dates of programs	Total number of years
1958, 1961, 1976(2), 1982–83	6

n.a. = not applicable

Notes: Summary of private forecasts for 2009 in *italics*. Banking crisis years shown in *italics* indicate that the episode was not deemed to be a systemic crisis.

**Figure 2.57b   South Africa: Private capital inflows from the United
Kingdom and banking crises, 1865–1895**

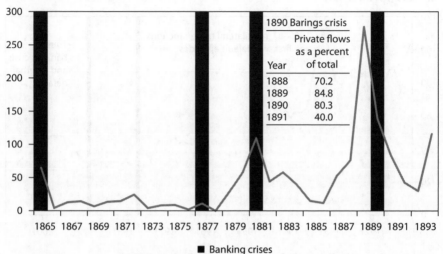

capital flows as a percent of exports

1890 Barings crisis	
	Private flows as a percent
Year	of total
1888	70.2
1889	84.8
1890	80.3
1891	40.0

■ Banking crises

Sources: Stone (1999), Reinhart and Rogoff (2009) and sources cited therein.

Figure 2.58a   Spain: Short-term loans to the Crown and defaults, 1601–79

billions of ducats, three-year sum

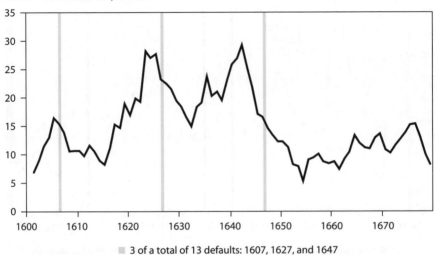

 3 of a total of 13 defaults: 1607, 1627, and 1647

Sources: Reinhart and Rogoff (2009) and sources cited therein.

Table 2.58a   Spain: Domestic default/restructuring, external default, banking crises, and hyperinflation, 1550–1799

External default/ restructuring	Duration (in years)	Domestic default/ restructuring	Banking crisis dates (first year)	Hyper-inflation dates	Share of years in external default	Share of years in inflation crisis
1557–60	4	1557–60	n.a.	n.a.	n.a.	
1575–77	3	1575–77				
1596–97	2	1596–97				
1607	1					
1627	1					
1647	1					
Number of episodes:						
6		3	0	0		

n.a. = not applicable

Figure 2.58b Spain: Central government (domestic plus external) debt, default, and banking crises, 1850–2009

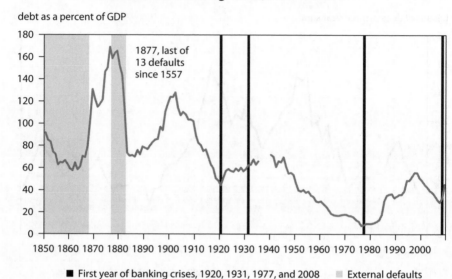

debt as a percent of GDP

1877, last of 13 defaults since 1557

■ First year of banking crises, 1920, 1931, 1977, and 2008   ▨ External defaults

Sources: Reinhart and Rogoff (2009) and sources cited therein.

Table 2.58b Spain: Default, restructuring, banking crises, growth collapses, and IMF programs, 1800–2009

External default/ restructuring	Duration (in years)	Domestic default/ restructuring	Banking crisis dates (first year)	Hyper-inflation dates	Share of years in external default	Share of years in inflation crisis	5 worst output collapses, year (decline)
1809	1	1936–39	1814	n.a.	23.8	3.8	1868 (10.1)
1820	1		1829				1874 (8.4)
1831–34	4		1846				1896 (8.0)
1837–67	31		1920				1936 (22.3)
1851	—		1931				1937 (8.3)
1877–82	7		1977				
Number of episodes:			2008				
6		0	6	0			

Memorandum item on IMF programs, 1952–2009
Dates of programs   Total number of years
1959, 1960, 1978   3

n.a. = not applicable

Figure 2.58c Spain: Total (public and private) capital inflows from the United Kingdom and banking crises, 1865–1913

capital flows as a percent of exports, three-year sum

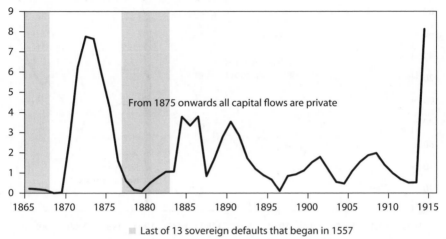

From 1875 onwards all capital flows are private

■ Last of 13 sovereign defaults that began in 1557

Sources: Stone (1999), Reinhart and Rogoff (2009) and sources cited therein.

Figure 2.58d Spain banking survey: Domestic credit, default, and banking crises, 1970–2008

credit outstanding at end of period as a percent of GDP, 4-quarter moving average

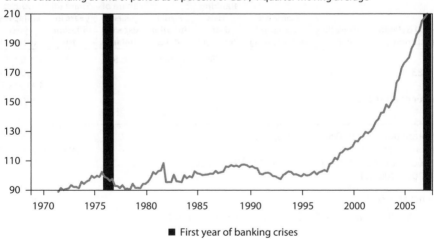

■ First year of banking crises

Notes: For periods where no quarterly nominal GDP is available, a moving-average interpolation method is used.

Sources: International Monetary Fund, *International Financial Statistics;* Reinhart and Rogoff (2009) and sources cited therein.

Figure 2.59 Sri Lanka: Central government (domestic plus external) debt, default, and banking crises, 1950–2009

debt as a percent of GDP

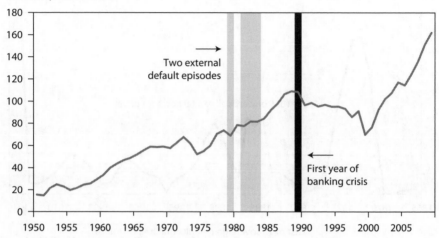

Sources: Reinhart and Rogoff (2009) and sources cited therein.

Table 2.59 Sri Lanka: Default, restructuring, banking crises, growth collapses, and IMF programs, 1948–2009

External default/ restructuring	Duration (in years)	Domestic default/ restructuring	Banking crisis dates (first year)	Hyper- inflation dates	Share of years in external default	Share of years in inflation crisis	4 worst output collapses, year (decline)
1979	1	1996	1989	n.a.	6.5	3.2	1918 (−6.5)
1981–83	3						1930 (4.0)
							1935 (5.2)
Number of episodes:							1944 (5.5)
2		1	1	0			

Memorandum item on IMF programs, 1952–2009
Dates of programs
1965–66, 1968–69, 1971, 1974, 1977, 1979, 1983, 1988, 1991, 2001, 2003(2)

Total number of years
14

n.a. = not applicable

Sources: Pre-World War II real GDP: Bassino and van del Eng (2006).

Figure 2.60a Sweden: Central government (domestic plus external) debt, default, and banking crises, 1719–2009

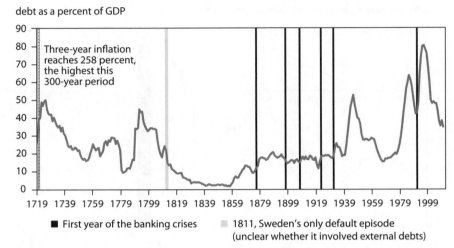

debt as a percent of GDP

■ First year of the banking crises

1811, Sweden's only default episode (unclear whether it involved external debts)

Notes: Prices are far more volatile during pre–World War II. For this reason, and owing to the fact that deflation is about as likely as inflation prior to the rise of fiat money, we also examine the evolution of (smoother) three-year changes in the price level.

Sources: Fregert and Gustafsson (2008); Reinhart and Rogoff (2009) and sources cited therein.

Table 2.60 Sweden: Default, restructuring, banking crises, growth collapses, and IMF programs, 1800–2009

External default/ restructuring	Duration (in years)	Domestic default/ restructuring	Banking crisis dates (first year)	Hyper-inflation dates	Share of years in external default	Share of years in inflation crisis	5 worst output collapses, year (decline)[1]
1811	1	n.a.	1811	n.a.	0.5	1.9	1826 (8.9)
			1876				1838 (5.7)
			1897				1861 (5.7)
			1907				1921 (3.7)
			1922				*2009 (4.2)*
			1931				
			1991				
Number of episodes:							
1		0	7	0			

Memorandum item on IMF programs, 1952–2009
Dates of programs   Total number of years
None   0

n.a. = not applicable

1. Excludes World Wars I and II.

Notes: Summary of private forecasts for 2009 in *italics*.

Figure 2.60b   Sweden banking survey: Domestic credit, default and banking crises, 1970–2008

credit outstanding at end of period as a percent of GDP

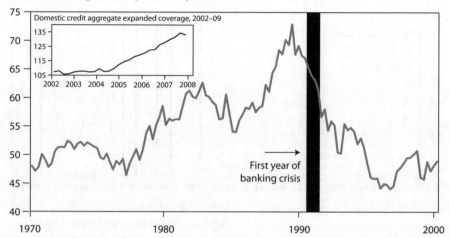

Sources: International Monetary Fund, *International Financial Statistics;* Reinhart and Rogoff (2009) and sources cited therein.

Figure 2.61   Switzerland: Central government (domestic plus external) debt and banking crises, 1880–2009

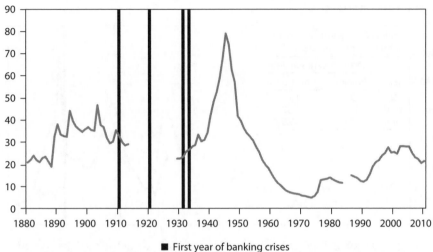

debt as a percent of GDP

■ First year of banking crises

Sources: Reinhart and Rogoff (2009) and sources cited therein.

Table 2.61   Switzerland: Default, restructuring, banking crises, growth collapses, and IMF programs, 1800–2009

External default/ restructuring	Duration (in years)	Domestic default/ restructuring	Banking crisis dates (first year)	Hyper- inflation dates	Share of years in external default	Share of years in inflation crisis	5 worst output collapses, year (decline)[1]
n.a.	n.a.	n.a.	1870	n.a.	n.a.		1854 (11.1)
			1910				1860 (13.0)
			1921				1867 (12.1)
			1931				1877 (9.7)
Number of episodes:			1933				1975 (7.3)
0		0	5	0			

Memorandum item on IMF programs, 1952–2009
Dates of programs
None

Total number of years
0

n.a. = not applicable

1. Excludes World Wars I and II.

Sources: Pre-World War II real GDP: Bassino and van del Eng (2006).

Figure 2.62a Thailand: Public (domestic and external) and external (public and private) debts, near-default, and banking crises, 1913–2009

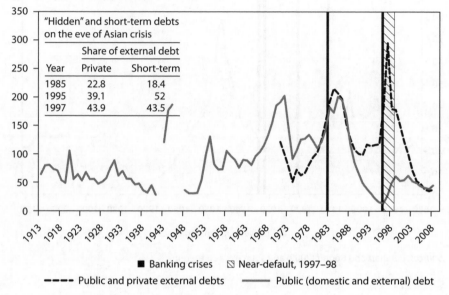

debt as a percent of exports

"Hidden" and short-term debts on the eve of Asian crisis		
	Share of external debt	
Year	Private	Short-term
1985	22.8	18.4
1995	39.1	52
1997	43.9	43.5

■ Banking crises ☒ Near-default, 1997–98

‒‒‒‒ Public and private external debts ——— Public (domestic and external) debt

Sources: Reinhart and Rogoff (2009) and sources cited therein.

Table 2.62 Thailand: Default, restructuring, banking crises, growth collapses, and IMF programs, 1800–2009

External default/ restructuring	Duration (in years)	Domestic default/ restructuring	Banking crisis dates (first year)	Hyper-inflation dates	Share of years in external default	Share of years in inflation crisis	5 worst output collapses, year (decline)
1997–98	"near" 2	n.a.	1983	n.a.	0	9	1919 (4.2)
			1996				1942 (9.0)
							1945 (6.8)
Number of episodes:							1998 (10.5)
0		0	2	0			*2009 (2.3)*

Memorandum item on IMF programs, 1952–2009
Dates of programs   Total number
1978, 1981–82, 1985, 1997   5

n.a. = not applicable

Notes: Summary of private forecasts for 2009 in *italics*. Near-defaults (not counted in total) are in *italics*.

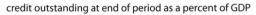

Figure 2.62b Thailand banking survey: Domestic credit and banking crises, 1970–2008

credit outstanding at end of period as a percent of GDP

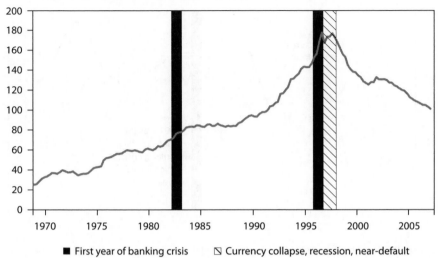

■ First year of banking crisis   ◨ Currency collapse, recession, near-default

Sources: International Monetary Fund, *International Financial Statistics;* Reinhart and Rogoff (2009) and sources cited therein.

Figure 2.63 Tunisia: External (public plus private) debt, default, and banking crises, 1970–2009

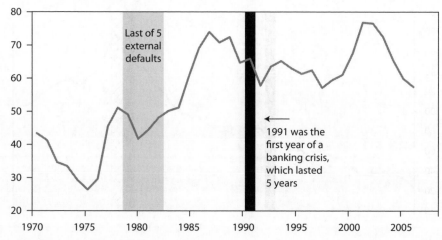

debt as a percent of GDP

Sources: Reinhart and Rogoff (2009) and sources cited therein.

Table 2.63 Tunisia: Default, restructuring, banking crises, growth collapses, and IMF programs, 1956–2009

External default/ restructuring	Duration (in years)	Domestic default/ restructuring	Banking crisis dates (first year)	Hyper-inflation dates	Share of years in external default	Share of years in inflation crisis	3 worst output collapses, year (decline)
1867–70	4	n.a.	1991	n.a.	13	0	1955 (5.1)
1956	1						1957 (4.1)
1958	1						1959 (4.2)
1963	1						
1979–82	4						
Number of episodes:							
5		0	1	0			

Memorandum item on IMF programs, 1952–2009
Dates of programs
1964–67, 1969–70, 1986, 1988

Total number
8

n.a. = not applicable

Figure 2.64a Turkey: External public debt, default, and banking crises, 1854–2009

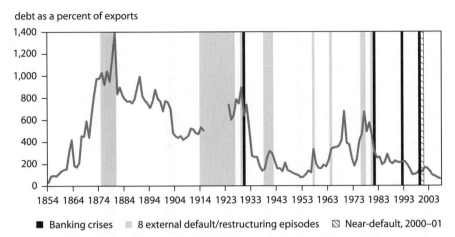

debt as a percent of exports

- ■ Banking crises   ▨ 8 external default/restructuring episodes   ⊠ Near-default, 2000–01

Sources: Pamuk (1995), Reinhart and Rogoff (2009) and sources cited therein.

Table 2.64   Turkey: Default, restructuring, banking crises, growth collapses, and IMF programs, 1800–2009 (calculations since independence— 1923, reported)

External default/ restructuring	Duration (in years)	Domestic default/ restructuring	Banking crisis dates (first year)	Hyper-inflation dates	Share of years in external default	Share of years in inflation crisis	5 worst output collapses, year (decline)[1]
1876–81	6	n.a.	1931	n.a.	19.5	35.6	1927 (9.1)
1915–28	14		1982				1932 (6.0)
1931–32	2		*1991*				1994 (5.5)
1940–43	4		2000				2001 (5.7)
1959	1						*2009 (5.6)*
1965	1						
1978–79	2						
1982	1						
2000–01 (near-default)	2						
Number of episodes: 8		0	4	0			

Memorandum item on IMF programs, 1952–2009
Dates of programs
1961–70, 1978–80, 1983–84, 1994, 1999, 2002

Total number
18

n.a. = not applicable

1. Excludes World Wars I and II.

Notes: Summary of private forecasts for 2009 in *italics*. Near-default (*italics*) not counted in total. Banking crisis years shown in *italics* indicate that the episode was not deemed to be a systemic crisis.

Figure 2.64b   Turkey: External public and private debts, default, near-default, and banking crises, 1970–2009

debt as a percent of GDP

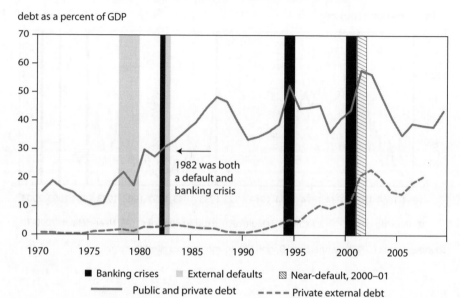

Sources: Reinhart and Rogoff (2009) and sources cited therein.

Figure 2.65a   United Kingdom: Central government debt, restructurings, and banking crises, 1692–2009

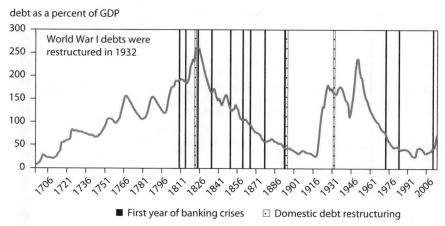

debt as a percent of GDP

■ First year of banking crises   ⊡ Domestic debt restructuring

Sources: UKpublicspending (2010), Reinhart and Rogoff (2009) and sources cited therein.

Table 2.65   United Kingdom: Default, restructuring, banking crises, growth collapses, and IMF programs, 1800–2009

External default/ restructuring	Duration (in years)	Domestic default/ restructuring	Banking crisis dates (first year)	Hyper-inflation dates	Share of years in external default	Share of years in inflation crisis	5 worst output collapses, year (decline)[1]
n.a.	n.a.	1822	1810	n.a.	n.a.	2.4	1919 (10.9)
		1834	1815				1920 (6.0)
		1888–89	1825				1921 (8.1)
		1932	1837				1931 (5.1)
			1847				*2009 (4.9)*
			1857				
			1866				
			1878				
			1890				
			1974				
			1984				
			2007				
Number of episodes:							
0		4	12	0			

Memorandum item on IMF programs, 1952–2009	
Dates of programs	Total
1956–58, 1961–64, 1967, 1969, 1975, 1977	11

n.a. = not applicable

1. Excludes World Wars I and II.

Notes: Summary of private forecasts for 2009 in *italics*. Banking crisis years shown in *italics* indicate that the episode was not deemed to be a systemic crisis.

Figure 2.65b   United Kingdom banking survey: Domestic credit and banking crises, 1970–2008

credit outstanding at end of period as a percent of GDP

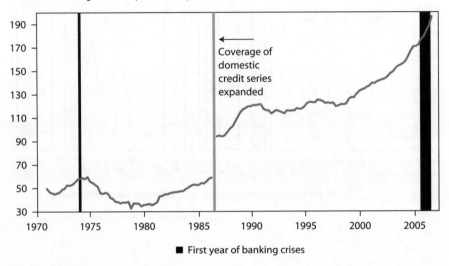

■ First year of banking crises

Sources: International Monetary Fund, *International Financial Statistics;* Reinhart and Rogoff (2009) and sources cited therein.

Figure 2.66a United States: Central government debt, default, and banking crises, 1790–2009

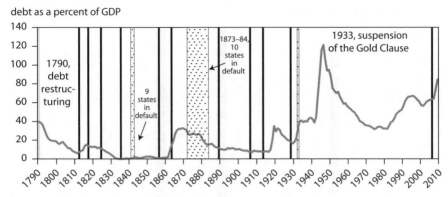

debt as a percent of GDP

■ First year of banking crises   ⊡ Domestic default/debt restructuring   ▨ External default, 1790

Sources: Reinhart and Rogoff (2009) and sources cited therein.

Table 2.66 United States: Default, restructuring, banking crises, growth collapses, and IMF programs, 1790–2009

External default/ restructuring	Duration (in years)	Domestic default/ restructuring	Banking crisis dates (first year)	Hyper-inflation dates	Share of years in external default	Share of years in inflation crisis	5 worst output collapses, year (decline)[1]
1790	1	1790	1814	n.a.	n.a.	1.4	1908 (10.8)
		1841–42	1818				1914 (7.7)
		1873–84	1836				1930 (8.6)
		1933	*1841*				1932 (13.1)
			1857				1946 (10.1)
			1861				
			1864				
			1873				
			1884				
			1890				
			1907				
			1914				
			1929				
			1984				
Number of episodes:			2007				
1		2	15	0			

Memorandum item on IMF programs, 1952–2009
Dates of programs   Total
1963–64   2

n.a. = not applicable

1. Excludes World Wars I and II.

Notes: The default of US states (*italics*) is not counted in the tally as the total number of episodes refers to sovereign credit events only. Banking crisis years shown in *italics* indicate that the episode was not deemed to be a systemic crisis.

Figure 2.66b   United States: Private capital inflows from the United Kingdom and banking crises, 1865–1914

capital flows as a percent of exports

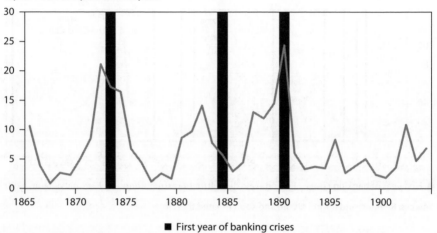

■ First year of banking crises

Sources: Stone (1999), Reinhart and Rogoff (2009) and sources cited therein.

Figure 2.66c   United States: Private debt outstanding, 1916–2009

end-of-period stock of debt as a percent of GDP

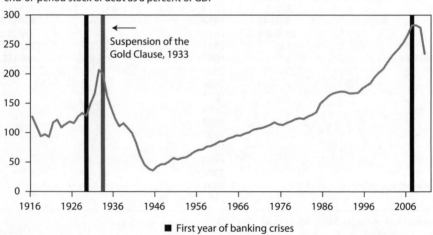

■ First year of banking crises

Notes: Data for 2009 are end of June. The Flow of Funds is reported for 1945–2009; prior to that the Historical Statistics of the United States series is scaled (down) to match the Flow of Funds data.

Sources: Historical Statistics of the United States, Flow of Funds, Board of Governors of the Federal Reserve; International Monetary Fund, *World Economic Outlook;* OECD; World Bank, *Global Development Finance;* and Reinhart and Rogoff (2009) and sources cited therein.

Figure 2.66d   United States banking survey: Domestic credit and banking crises, 1970–2008

credit outstanding at end of period as a percent of GDP

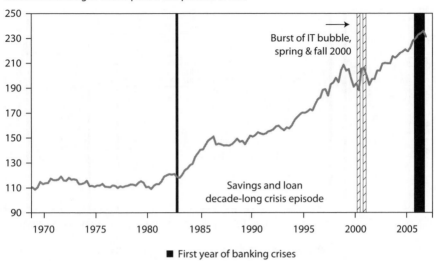

■ First year of banking crises

Sources: International Monetary Fund, *International Financial Statistics;* Reinhart and Rogoff (2009) and sources cited therein.

Figure 2.67a Uruguay: Public (domestic plus external) debt, default, restructuring, and banking crises, 1871–2009

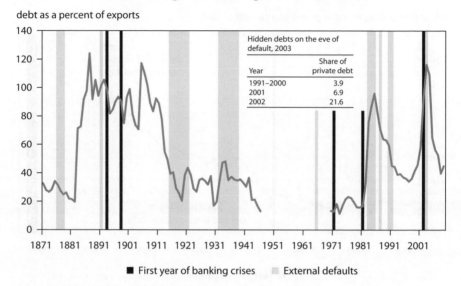

debt as a percent of exports

Hidden debts on the eve of default, 2003

Year	Share of private debt
1991–2000	3.9
2001	6.9
2002	21.6

■ First year of banking crises ▨ External defaults

Notes: For the period 1871–1914 only external debt data are available. Domestic debts (only a few observations are available) were negligible during this period.

Sources: Reinhart and Rogoff (2009) and sources cited therein.

Table 2.67 Uruguay: Default, restructuring, banking crises, growth collapses, and IMF programs, 1811–2009

External default/ restructuring	Duration (in years)	Domestic default/ restructuring	Banking crisis dates (first year)	Hyper-inflation dates	Share of years in external default	Share of years in inflation crisis	6 worst output collapses, year (decline)
1876–78	3	1932–37	1893	n.a.	13	18	1905 (10.1)
1891	1		1898				1914 (16.7)
1915–21	7		1971				1920 (12.8)
1932–38	7		1981				1931 (17.3)
1965	1		2002				1933 (12.5)
1983–85	3						1982 (9.3)
1987	1						
1990–91	2						
2003	1						
Number of episodes:							
9		1	5	0			

Memorandum item on IMF programs, 1952–2009
Dates of programs
1961–62, 1966, 1968, 1970, 1972, 1975–77, 1979–81, 1983, 1985, 1990, 1992, 1997, 1999–2002

Total
21

n.a. = not applicable

Figure 2.67b Uruguay: Total (private and public) capital inflows from the United Kingdom and default and banking crises, 1865–1914

capital flows as a percent of exports, three-year sum

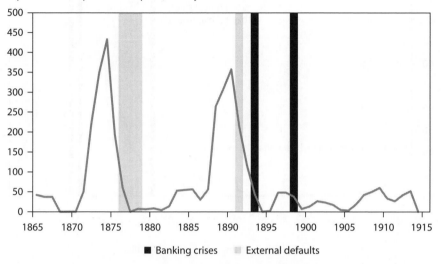

Sources: Stone (1999), Reinhart and Rogoff (2009) and sources cited therein.

Figure 2.68 Venezuela: Central government (domestic plus external) debt, default, and banking crises, 1921–2009

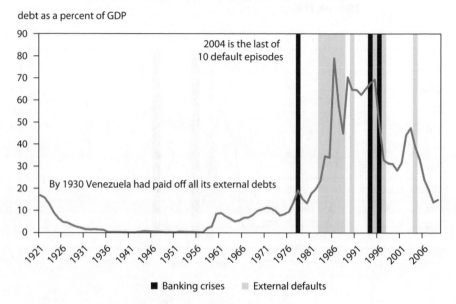

debt as a percent of GDP

Sources: Reinhart and Rogoff (2009) and sources cited therein.

Table 2.68 Venezuela: Default, restructuring, banking crises, growth collapses, and IMF programs, 1829–2009

External default/ restructuring	Duration (in years)	Domestic default/ restructuring	Banking crisis dates (first year)	Hyper-inflation dates	Share of years in external default	Share of years in inflation crisis	5 worst output collapses, year (decline)
1826–40	15	1995–97	1978	n.a.	35.9	11	1914 (12.6)
1848–59	12	1998	1993				1931 (19.2)
1860–62	3						1942 (12.6)
1865–81	17						1989 (8.6)
1892	1						2002 (8.9)
1898–1905	8						
1983–88	6						
1990	1						
1995–97	3						
2004–05	2						
Number of episodes:							
10		2	2	0			

Memorandum item on IMF programs, 1952–2009
Dates of programs   Total number
1960, 1989, 1996   3

n.a. = not applicable

Figure 2.69 Zambia: External (public plus private) debt, default, and banking crises, 1970–2009

debt as a percent of GDP

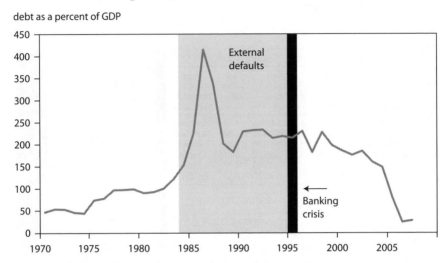

Sources: Reinhart and Rogoff (2009) and sources cited therein.

Table 2.69 Zambia: Default, restructuring, banking crises, growth collapses, and IMF programs, 1964–2009

External default/ restructuring	Duration (in years)	Domestic default/ restructuring	Banking crisis dates (first year)	Hyper- inflation dates	Share of years in external default	Share of years in inflation crisis	3 worst output collapses, year (decline)
1983–94	12	n.a.	1995	n.a.	24	40	1966 (5.5) 1977 (4.9)
Number of episodes:							1994 (13.3)
1		0	1	0			

Memorandum item on IMF programs, 1952–2009
Dates of programs   Total
1973, 1976, 1978, 1981, 1983–84, 1986, 1995(2), 1999, 2004, 2008   12

n.a. = not applicable

Figure 2.70 Zimbabwe: External (public plus private) debt, default, restructuring, hyperinflation, and banking crises, 1970–2009

debt as a percent of GDP

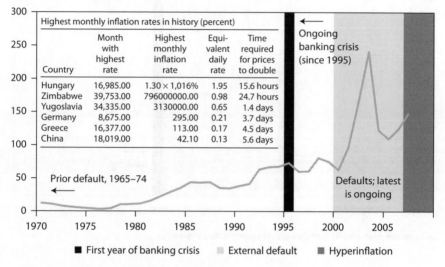

Highest monthly inflation rates in history (percent)

Country	Month with highest rate	Highest monthly inflation rate	Equi-valent daily rate	Time required for prices to double
Hungary	16,985.00	1.30 × 1,016%	1.95	15.6 hours
Zimbabwe	39,753.00	796000000.00	0.98	24.7 hours
Yugoslavia	34,335.00	3130000.00	0.65	1.4 days
Germany	8,675.00	295.00	0.21	3.7 days
Greece	16,377.00	113.00	0.17	4.5 days
China	18,019.00	42.10	0.13	5.6 days

Ongoing banking crisis (since 1995)

Prior default, 1965–74

Defaults; latest is ongoing

■ First year of banking crisis   ▨ External default   ■ Hyperinflation

Sources: Hanke (2008), Reinhart and Rogoff (2009) and sources cited therein.

Table 2.70 Zimbabwe: Default, restructuring, banking crises, growth collapses, hyperinflation, and IMF programs, 1965–2009

External default/ restructuring	Duration (in years)	Domestic default/ restructuring	Banking crisis dates (first year)	Hyper-inflation dates	Share of years in external default	Share of years in inflation crisis	5 worst output collapses, year (decline)
1965–74	10	2006	1995	2006–09	40	40	1977 (8.0)
2000–09	10						1992 (8.4)
							2000 (7.3)
Number of episodes:							2003 (10.4)
2		1	1	1			2008 (14.1)

Memorandum item on IMF programs, 1952–2009
Dates of programs
1981, 1983, 1992 (3), 1998, 1999

Total
7

About the Authors

Carmen M. Reinhart is the new Dennis Weatherstone Senior Fellow at the Peterson Institute for International Economics. She was previously professor of economics and director of the Center for International Economics at the University of Maryland. She was chief economist and vice president at the investment bank Bear Stearns in the 1980s and spent several years at the International Monetary Fund. She is a research associate at the National Bureau of Economic Research, research fellow at the Centre for Economic Policy Research, and member of the Congressional Budget Office Panel of Economic Advisers and Council on Foreign Relations. She has served on many editorial boards and has frequently testified before Congress. Reinhart's work has helped to inform the understanding of financial crises for over a decade. Her numerous papers on macroeconomics, international finance, and trade have been published in leading scholarly journals. She is the recipient of the 2010 TIAA-CREF Paul A. Samuelson Award. Her best-selling book (with Kenneth S. Rogoff) entitled *This Time is Different: Eight Centuries of Financial Folly*, which has been translated into 13 languages, documents the striking similarities of the recurring booms and busts that have characterized financial history. She received her PhD from Columbia University.

Kenneth S. Rogoff is a member of the Peterson Institute for International Economics Advisory Committee and the Thomas D. Cabot Professor of Public Policy and Professor of Economics at Harvard University. He also served as chief economist and director of research at the International Monetary Fund (2001–03). He is the recipient of the 2010 TIAA-CREF Paul A. Samuelson Award.

His publications include *This Time is Different: Eight Centuries of Financial Folly*, *Handbook of International Economics* Volume III, and *Foundations of International Macroeconomics*. Rogoff is a frequent commentator for NPR, the *Wall Street Journal*, and the *Financial Times*.

Index

Other Publications from the Peterson Institute for International Economics

10 Bank Lending to Developing Countries: The Policy Alternatives* C. Fred Bergsten, William R. Cline, and John Williamson
April 1985 ISBN 0-88132-032-3

11 Trading for Growth: The Next Round of Trade Negotiations*
Gary Clyde Hufbauer and Jeffrey J. Schott
September 1985 ISBN 0-88132-033-1

12 Financial Intermediation Beyond the Debt Crisis* Donald R. Lessard and John Williamson
September 1985 ISBN 0-88132-021-8

13 The United States-Japan Economic Problem* C. Fred Bergsten and William R. Cline
Oct. 1985, 2d ed. January 1987
ISBN 0-88132-060-9

14 Deficits and the Dollar: The World Economy at Risk* Stephen Marris
Dec. 1985, 2d ed. November 1987
ISBN 0-88132-067-6

15 Trade Policy for Troubled Industries*
Gary Clyde Hufbauer and Howard F. Rosen
March 1986 ISBN 0-88132-020-X

16 The United States and Canada: The Quest for Free Trade* Paul Wonnacott, with an appendix by John Williamson
March 1987 ISBN 0-88132-056-0

17 Adjusting to Success: Balance of Payments Policy in the East Asian NICs*
Bela Balassa and John Williamson
June 1987, rev. April 1990
ISBN 0-88132-101-X

18 Mobilizing Bank Lending to Debtor Countries* William R. Cline
June 1987 ISBN 0-88132-062-5

19 Auction Quotas and United States Trade Policy* C. Fred Bergsten, Kimberly Ann Elliott, Jeffrey J. Schott, and Wendy E. Takacs
September 1987 ISBN 0-88132-050-1

20 Agriculture and the GATT: Rewriting the Rules* Dale E. Hathaway
September 1987 ISBN 0-88132-052-8

21 Anti-Protection: Changing Forces in United States Trade Politics*
I. M. Destler and John S. Odell
September 1987 ISBN 0-88132-043-9

22 Targets and Indicators: A Blueprint for the International Coordination of Economic Policy John Williamson and Marcus H. Miller
September 1987 ISBN 0-88132-051-X

23 Capital Flight: The Problem and Policy Responses* Donald R. Lessard and John Williamson
December 1987 ISBN 0-88132-059-5

24 United States-Canada Free Trade: An Evaluation of the Agreement*
Jeffrey J. Schott
April 1988 ISBN 0-88132-072-2

25 Voluntary Approaches to Debt Relief*
John Williamson
Sept. 1988, rev. May 1 ISBN 0-88132-098-6

26 American Trade Adjustment: The Global Impact* William R. Cline
March 1989 ISBN 0-88132-095-1

27 More Free Trade Areas?* Jeffrey J. Schott
May 1989 ISBN 0-88132-085-4

28 The Progress of Policy Reform in Latin America* John Williamson
January 1990 ISBN 0-88132-100-1

29 The Global Trade Negotiations: What Can Be Achieved?* Jeffrey J. Schott
September 1990 ISBN 0-88132-137-0

30 Economic Policy Coordination: Requiem for Prologue?* Wendy Dobson
April 1991 ISBN 0-88132-102-8

31 The Economic Opening of Eastern Europe*
John Williamson
May 1991 ISBN 0-88132-186-9

32 Eastern Europe and the Soviet Union in the World Economy* Susan Collins and Dani Rodrik
May 1991 ISBN 0-88132-157-5

33 African Economic Reform: The External Dimension* Carol Lancaster
June 1991 ISBN 0-88132-096-X

34 Has the Adjustment Process Worked?*
Paul R. Krugman
October 1991 ISBN 0-88132-116-8

35 From Soviet DisUnion to Eastern Economic Community?* Oleh Havrylyshyn and John Williamson
October 1991 ISBN 0-88132-192-3

36 Global Warming: The Economic Stakes*
William R. Cline
May 1992 ISBN 0-88132-172-9

37 Trade and Payments after Soviet Disintegration* John Williamson
June 1992 ISBN 0-88132-173-7

38 Trade and Migration: NAFTA and Agriculture* Philip L. Martin
October 1993 ISBN 0-88132-201-6

39 The Exchange Rate System and the IMF: A Modest Agenda Morris Goldstein
June 1995 ISBN 0-88132-219-9

40 What Role for Currency Boards?
John Williamson
September 1995 ISBN 0-88132-222-9

41 Predicting External Imbalances for the United States and Japan* William R. Cline
September 1995 ISBN 0-88132-220-2

42 Standards and APEC: An Action Agenda*
John S. Wilson
October 1995 ISBN 0-88132-223-7

43 Fundamental Tax Reform and Border Tax Adjustments* Gary Clyde Hufbauer
January 1996 ISBN 0-88132-225-3

44 Global Telecom Talks: A Trillion Dollar Deal* Ben A. Petrazzini
June 1996 ISBN 0-88132-230-X

45 WTO 2000: Setting the Course for World Trade Jeffrey J. Schott
September 1996 ISBN 0-88132-234-2

46 The National Economic Council: A Work in Progress* I. M. Destler
November 1996 ISBN 0-88132-239-3

WORKS IN PROGRESS

Peterson
Institute for
International
Economics

News

September 9, 2011

Contact: Katharine Keenan (202) 454-1334

SENIOR FELLOW CARMEN M. REINHART WINS COUNCIL ON FOREIGN RELATIONS' ARTHUR ROSS BOOK AWARD

WASHINGTON—The Peterson Institute for International Economics is pleased to announce that Senior Fellow Carmen M. Reinhart, along with her coauthor Kenneth S. Rogoff, have won the Council on Foreign Relations' tenth annual Arthur Ross Book Award for their trailblazing study, *This Time is Different: Eight Centuries of Financial Folly.* Their provocative study is widely quoted and has increasingly informed the policy discussion surrounding the current financial and economic crisis.

"We at the Institute are enormously proud of Carmen's contribution to the understanding of one of the most critical issues facing the world today and its potential to help guide us out of the crisis," said C. Fred Bergsten, director of the Peterson Institute. Reinhart has been Dennis Weatherstone Senior Fellow since joining the Peterson Institute from the University of Maryland in November 2010.

This Time is Different provides a comprehensive analysis of financial crises of the last 800 years. In each instance, contemporary observers asserted that their particular circumstances were unique, bearing little resemblance to past experiences and therefore suggesting that the old rules no longer applied. Reinhart and Rogoff, who is a professor of economics at Harvard, present evidence to the contrary and powerfully demonstrate remarkable similarities in sovereign defaults, bank failures and other financial disruptions over many centuries. They find the frequency, duration and severity of financial crises to be strikingly consistent. However, they say, a sort of amnesia occurs among policy makers that contributes to their complacency and to the recurrence of crises.

The Arthur Ross Book Award is a prestigious prize for a book on international affairs. It was endowed by Arthur Ross in 2001 to honor nonfiction works, in English or translation, that merit special attention for bringing forth new information that changes the world's understanding of events or problems and leads to new insights that help resolve foreign and economic policy problems. The winner receives $15,000. An award ceremony took place on September 8 in New York.

1750 Massachusetts Avenue, NW   Washington, DC 20036-1903   Tel 202.328.9000   Fax 202.659.3225   www.piie.com

About the Peterson Institute

The **Peter G. Peterson Institute for International Economics** is a private, nonprofit, nonpartisan research institution devoted to the study of international economic policy. Since 1981 the Institute has provided timely and objective analysis of, and concrete solutions to, a wide range of international economic problems. It is one of the very few economics think tanks that are widely regarded as "nonpartisan" by the press and "neutral" by the US Congress, its research staff is cited by the quality media more than that of any other such institution. Support is provided by a wide range of charitable foundations, private corporations and individual donors, and from earnings on the Institute's publications and capital fund. It moved into its award-winning new building in 2001, and celebrated its 25th anniversary in 2006 and adopted its new name at that time, having previously been the Institute for International Economics.

2

DISTRIBUTORS OUTSIDE THE UNITED STATES

**Australia, New Zealand,
and Papua New Guinea**
D. A. Information Services
648 Whitehorse Road
Mitcham, Victoria 3132, Australia
Tel: 61-3-9210-7777
Fax: 61-3-9210-7788
Email: service@dadirect.com.au
www.dadirect.com.au

India, Bangladesh, Nepal, and Sri Lanka
Viva Books Private Limited
Mr. Vinod Vasishtha
4737/23 Ansari Road
Daryaganj, New Delhi 110002
India
Tel: 91-11-4224-2200
Fax: 91-11-4224-2240
Email: viva@vivagroupindia.net
www.vivagroupindia.com

**Mexico, Central America, South America,
and Puerto Rico**
US PubRep, Inc.
311 Dean Drive
Rockville, MD 20851
Tel: 301-838-9276
Fax: 301-838-9278
Email: c.falk@ieee.org

**Asia (*Brunei, Burma, Cambodia, China,
Hong Kong, Indonesia, Korea, Laos, Malaysia,
Philippines, Singapore, Taiwan, Thailand,
and Vietnam*)**
East-West Export Books (EWEB)
University of Hawaii Press
2840 Kolowalu Street
Honolulu, Hawaii 96822-1888
Tel: 808-956-8830
Fax: 808-988-6052
Email: eweb@hawaii.edu

Canada
Renouf Bookstore
5369 Canotek Road, Unit 1
Ottawa, Ontario KlJ 9J3, Canada
Tel: 613-745-2665
Fax: 613-745-7660
www.renoufbooks.com

Japan
United Publishers Services Ltd.
1-32-5, Higashi-shinagawa
Shinagawa-ku, Tokyo 140-0002
Japan
Tel: 81-3-5479-7251
Fax: 81-3-5479-7307
Email: purchasing@ups.co.jp
*For trade accounts only. Individuals will find
Institute books in leading Tokyo bookstores.*

Middle East
MERIC
2 Bahgat Ali Street, El Masry Towers
Tower D, Apt. 24
Zamalek, Cairo
Egypt
Tel. 20-2-7633824
Fax: 20-2-7369355
Email: mahmoud_fouda@mericonline.com
www.mericonline.com

**United Kingdom, Europe
(*including Russia and Turkey*), Africa,
and Israel**
The Eurospan Group
c/o Turpin Distribution
Pegasus Drive
Stratton Business Park
Biggleswade, Bedfordshire
SG18 8TQ
United Kingdom
Tel: 44 (0) 1767-604972
Fax: 44 (0) 1767-601640
Email: eurospan@turpin-distribution.com
www.eurospangroup.com/bookstore

**Visit our website at:
www.piie.com
E-mail orders to:
petersonmail@presswarehouse.com**